about this research review

research in practice aims to make it easier for those who deliver services to children and families – whether they work in local authorities, voluntary organisations, health settings, national government organisations or any of their local partner agencies – to access reliable research, distilled and translated with their particular needs in mind. This series of research reviews covers key practice questions identified by practitioners, and key research strategy issues identified by planners and policy makers. The National Youth Agency is delighted to be joint commissioners of this review – working in partnership with **research in practice** fits absolutely with our central mission to support young people to achieve their full potential. We see this review as an important way of making a positive contribution to the government's new focus on youth, by equipping agencies and practitioners with a resource to help them support local developments around this key agenda.

As you will read in this review, education and fulfilling work are key routes to leaving or avoiding social exclusion. Those young people who experience adversity can find the transition from school to work very hard indeed. We are, however, in a time of change and development. The introduction of diplomas and new support systems begin to address some the challenges faced by young people in accessing a relevant educational offer. The current Education and Skills Bill proposes raising the age of participation in education and training to 18 by 2015, through a phased process. The intention is that 100 per cent of young people participate in high-quality and relevant provision. The bill recognises the contribution of the non-formal sector and further clarification is expected in subsequent guidance. Future plans are also being developed which re-emphasise the role of the local authority in working with national bodies and regional/local providers to secure a more coherent offer to our young people.

Already, reducing the number of young people who are NEET is the National Indicator most frequently listed in the current round of Local Area Agreements. This statement of wholehearted commitment to young people and their future provides a fantastic opportunity to improve services and outcomes and provides an excellent platform from which to build the new arrangements. The local authority is well placed to unlock the full contribution of the non-formal system – the network of voluntary and community providers, integrated youth support and development services and other relevant organisations, such as libraries. This is all good news for young people who will be able to access a broader set of opportunities to enrich and deepen their learning, in places and at times that are comfortable, and supported by skilled and significant adults. For those young people who have complex and fractured lives, this can be their first real opportunity to engage.

As we move forward it is essential that we learn from the past – what works and also what doesn't. This review makes a timely contribution to that understanding and should support managers and practitioners in the development of effective practice. The review's title, *One in Ten*, refers to the percentage of young people who are NEET at any one time – and this figure has proved, so far, very difficult to shift downwards. We look forward to working with others to turn this curve in the right direction.

The aim of the review is to bring together available research and promising effective practice developments that are disparate and not already collated in another publication, to form an overview of the topic – young people not in education, employment or training. We hope that this review will be of use to commissioners, strategy teams, performance and quality assurance staff, trainers, managers and practitioners throughout children's services – and including those working in the police, youth justice and health services.

Celia Atherton   Viv McKee
Director of **research in practice**   Director of Policy and Research, NYA

QUALITY MARK This review has been peer-reviewed by a range of academics based in universities and service agencies, and by practitioners and others committed to the development of evidence-informed practice. Thanks are due to Peter Chell, Gill Cowan, Helen Evans, Sue Houlton, Tricia Jessiman, Bethia McNeil, Diana Onyango, Martin Pratt and David Pye.

We are grateful to the many other people who have been generous with their time and wisdom, sending us information and responding to our queries. Thanks to Pauline Benefield, Keith Bootle, Sally Booth, Liz Brown, Mark Christopher, Sailesh Devani, Hayley Dixon, Robin Douglas, Tony Graham, Richard Hartley, Steve Howell, Olly Newton, Chris Palmer, Louise Richards, Claire Shiels and Nick Whittingham.

The authors would like to pay special thanks to Tricia Jessiman, in addition to her peer review, for setting them on the right tracks for this review and for being a constant and willing source of information, advice and guidance.

In memory of Deborah Loeb
friend, colleague, inspiration

contents

Setting the scene

introduction

This review focuses on one important group of young people and families who are currently high on the national and local policy agenda. They are the young people who are described as **NEET**, meaning Not in Education, Employment or Training.

The topic was chosen in the normal **research in practice** way, by asking Partner Agencies to suggest current issues about which practitioners and managers would value summary information for their work. Young people who are NEET was the most popular topic suggested at the end of 2007, now mirrored in the priority given to this topic by local professional partnerships. In view of their lead role in policy and practice work with young people, The National Youth Agency was invited to jointly commission the review.

The young people who are or may become NEET affect us all in some way. They are the young people looking for work in our local shops and restaurants, they are the pupils struggling in our local schools, they are our children and young relatives and their friends.

The review highlights that:

- We are talking about some 189,000 young people who are NEET — more than enough to fill London's new Wembley Stadium twice over. It amounts to just under one in ten young people.
- Moving from school to work is more difficult to negotiate than moving from school to further education. Young people with personal or family problems are more likely to struggle at school, putting the option of further education beyond their reach. When these problems are compounded by non-participation in work or learning, the risk of social exclusion increases.
- The biggest proportion of young people who are NEET are aged 18 and this is also the group where least progress is being made.
- Non-formal learning can boost young people's self-confidence and have a knock-on effect in other areas of their life, leading for example to a reduction in inappropriate risk taking and the adoption of a more healthy lifestyle.
- The drive to meet targets can get in the way of going at a young person's pace and helping them develop important personal and social skills.
- Local initiatives demonstrate what it is possible to achieve for young people. 'Stuff happens' when the work is being done by or with the support of local champions whose approach pays careful heed to the messages from young people and their families about what will work best for them and why.

- There is cause for optimism about what might be achieved at the local level in that 115 of 150 local authorities have chosen reducing the number of young people who are NEET as a top priority under their new Local Area Agreement.[1]

The review draws on a wide range of publications and other sources. It does so in order to extract the messages that might help practitioners and managers improve their understanding of this group of vulnerable young people and families, and build on current endeavours to improve the life chances of those making the transition from compulsory education to young adulthood.

The review is intended for practitioners in all agencies working with and for children and families, and for managers, commissioners and others with strategic, operational and training responsibilities for the delivery of services to promote the Every Child Matters and associated programmes. It set out to explore the literature for answers to the questions posed by those working in the field, and to bring together in one place disparate information about available research and promising practice developments, to form an overview of the topic.

We hope the review will be of particular interest to those striving to be flexible in their work with young people, and whose starting point is to make services 'easier to access' rather than thinking of people as 'hard to engage'. We hope it will boost the work of those who take a broad view of their role in responding to the needs of individual young people and those close to them. And we hope it will help those who strive to create stronger links across different services so that young people's participation in learning can be promoted by shared professional understanding and a keen commitment to address the wide range of difficulties that can – and do – dash young people's hopes or temper their aspirations.

This is not a new agenda. Some of the initiatives being piloted and extended are revised versions of programmes that were tried and tested on our previous generation of young people. A decade ago, the government's seminal report about young people not participating in education, employment or training commented on the change that was needed to stem the adverse impact of lost time and opportunity on young people themselves, their community, and society as a whole.

For the majority, these are wasted and frustrating years that lead, inexorably, to lower pay and worse job prospects ... Young people need to be better prepared for adult life. [59]

---

[1] A Local Area Agreement (LAA) is a three-year agreement that sets out the priorities between central government and a local area. The main aim is to deliver better outcomes for local people and the starting point is usually a community strategy. In deciding its priorities each local authority must choose 35 out of 198 National Indicators to implement. Indicator 117 is about reducing the number of young people aged 16 to 18 who are NEET.

More recently, in heralding its renewed focus on young people who are NEET, the government acknowledged the challenge ahead.

The demands of the economy, and our ambition for social justice, mean that we must do more. We need excellence in education and training not just for some but for all young people ... We will ensure that those who are most at risk of not participating, and therefore with the most to gain, are not left to fall behind. [21]

a note about language and definitions

language

NEET is a short-hand term that came into being following the government's 1999 report *Bridging the Gap: New opportunities for 16-18 year olds not in education, employment or training*. The report, by the cross-departmental Social Exclusion Unit, was about the need for greater participation in 'education, employment or training' by young people who had left school [59]. Soon after publication, the term NEET was coined. It has been used widely ever since.

There is a debate about whether the term is appropriate, however. Opponents point to its negative and stigmatising connotation. They say it defines young people in terms of what they are not doing, rather than what they are achieving, and implies that their work or learning status alone defines their identity. In this sense the term is similar to the earlier term 'status zero', which had also come under fire as being derogatory [5]. What is considered particularly demeaning is using the short-hand term on its own, referring to young people as 'NEETs' rather than using the albeit longer phrase 'young people who are NEET'. Throughout the review, we have endeavoured to use language that is respectful to young people and their families.

definitions

The term NEET may slip easily off the tongue, but it is not so easy to define. This is because its use has developed in recent years, leaving some uncertainties about its precise meaning.

One variation is about age. The term is sometimes used to refer to young people and young adults up to age 24 – and the catchy term 'NEET generation' has even begun to appear in media discussions. But unless otherwise specified, in this review we use the term NEET in its more established sense – to refer to older teenagers aged 16 to 18.

Another change is reflected in the introduction of the term 'pre-NEET'. Technically, this could refer to any child or young person, of any age, who is at risk of not making a successful transition to education, employment or training. But the term is commonly used to describe young people aged 14 to 16 who, identified as being at risk of disengaging from education, need help to ensure that they become involved in some learning activity up to and beyond the official school-leaving age. This help to the under-16s is described as NEET *prevention*. It is different from NEET *reduction* which is the term used to describe the help for those who are over 16. We make some reference to young people who are pre-NEET in the review.

The young people we are talking about[2]

Karen – not engaged in work or learning

Karen is just 18. She was assessed at school as having special educational needs. She has never had a job and needed a work placement (preferably a paid job) in animal care so that she could start her college placement and then progress to qualifications in the care of small animals – a notoriously difficult area in which to find a work placement, let alone a paid job. However, Karen's contract with her personal adviser enabled an employer-accompanied visit to take place. This was to a local tourist centre. Karen was offered a trial in the animal section of the centre and was able to take up the college place.

Lucy – working, but with no opportunity for training

Lucy lives in a rural area. When the leaving care project engaged with her, she was working in a local restaurant. She was living at home and had a commitment to contribute to the household income. Lucy had always wanted to work in child care but did not know how to get going. As far as targets were concerned, she would count as a young person in EET as she was employed. But Lucy was not fulfilling her potential and really wanted a career in child care. As the leaving care project is about added value it was important to help Lucy resist settling for the first job that came her way.

The project helped her consider the available options. It liaised with her Connexions personal adviser and local agencies to see how best to support her. Lucy was helped to get a skills assessment from a local training provider, which led to an offer of a pre-employment course to address her basic skills needs. The project helped her sort out her entitlement to a cash allowance and a work experience placement through the local voluntary bureau and its contact with local schools and nurseries. All the agencies worked with Lucy to organise a programme of four days a week in placement and one in college, where Lucy sat in on a child care course to study the underpinning knowledge as part of her pre-employment programme. Lucy was nominated for an achievement award from her local authority.

Vicky – keen to train for the work she wants to do

Vicky met her personal adviser to discuss work and training options. She also met the local training provider. Vicky turned down the offer of a pre-employment programme on the grounds that her parents' income was too high for her to qualify for the weekly cash allowance that came with the programme and because she felt the programme would be too similar to full-time education. She also cancelled the place she had secured at the local further education college because her family would have had to pay £250 in bus fares during the course as well as buying hairdressing equipment. Her personal adviser commented: 'This isn't a high income family, just a regular, hardworking one.'

[2] The case examples in the review (about services or young people's experiences) are taken from reports from local authorities, Connexions and other agencies. Some services may no longer be operating in the way described, but the ideas behind them remain relevant.

the policy context

Youth unemployment was not a new concern in the late 1990s. But it assumed fresh prominence in the government's policy agenda after a programme of work by the Social Exclusion Unit[3] led in 1999 to the publication of its seminal report about the participation of 16- to 18-year-olds in education, employment and training – *Bridging the Gap* [59]. The report identified the adverse impact of non-participation on young people themselves and on their community and wider society.

impact on young people

Although it introduced the concept of young people who are NEET, the report did not assume this was the only (or even the key) problem facing that group. Nor did it assume that a young person's re-engagement in work or learning would fully answer their problems. These young people are often confronted with a complex range of barriers to success, many of which begin well before they reach their teens, and it is often very difficult to recover from this poor start in life. This complexity was re-affirmed six years later in the Social Exclusion Unit's report *Transitions: Young adults with complex needs* [53].

At the time of the Social Exclusion Unit's first report, only one in three 18-year-olds without a job, and fewer than one in four who were looking after their home or family, had reached or exceeded a qualification at Level 2 (the equivalent of GCSE grades A-C). Being NEET was also a strong indicator of teenage parenthood. Some young people's 'journeys' were also very muddled. Some were choosing or falling into an unsuitable college course and then dropping out. Worse still, some took a short-term job of poor quality with no training attached, interspersed with periods of no meaningful activity at all.

In the longer term, NEET status for six months or longer was a major predictor of unemployment at age 21 and beyond. Four-fifths of those out of work and education at age 16, 20 and 24 remained so at age 18, 24 and 29 respectively. When things went wrong for 16- to 18-year-olds, social exclusion in later life was disproportionately the result. They were much more likely to be unemployed, dependent on benefits, living in an unstable family structure, and depressed about their life.

impact on communities and society

The cumulative financial impact on society is high. In 2007, a report for the Prince's Trust estimated that youth unemployment was costing the UK economy £70 million a week in lost productivity – or more than £3.6 billion a year [45]. In addition, the government was paying out £20 million every week in Jobseeker's Allowance for 18- to 24-year-

---

[3] The Social Exclusion Unit was set up by the Prime Minister in 1997. It was replaced in June 2006 by the Social Exclusion Task Force. Whereas the SEU had a broad focus, the SETF aims to tackle the problems experienced by those facing the most entrenched and complex forms of exclusion. The SETF works with and across government departments to identify priorities and help test joined-up solutions to multiple and intergenerational problems.

olds. The report, which was based on research carried out by the Centre for Economic Performance at the London School of Economics, found that educational underachievement was also affecting the relative performance of the UK economy. The UK was reported to have between 10 and 25 per cent lower output per hour than France, Germany and the US – much of which could be attributed to 'a poorer level of skills and a shortfall in capital investment'.

Consequences beyond the purely financial were spelled out by the Social Exclusion Unit. Young people truanting from school were almost twice as likely as their peers to have used solvents and illicit drugs. Three-quarters of young men aged 16 and 17 coming before the youth courts were not in formal full-time activity. Young women who were NEET for more than six months between 16 and 18 were four times more likely to be a parent by age 21, and a third of young women who were teenage mothers had not been engaged in learning or work before becoming a parent. There was an impact over the generations, too, with young adults twice as likely to be out of work for over a year if their father had been out of work at age 16.

The report identified the changes that were needed. It also set these proposals for change in the context of offering a double dividend: 'getting things right' was presented as a moral as well as a business imperative. For young people, there was the chance to escape from the prospects of a lifetime of dead-end jobs, unemployment, poverty, ill-health and other kinds of social and economic exclusion. For society, there was the anticipated reduction in the financial burden stemming from the failure to help young people make a successful transition from being a child to becoming an independent adult.

So what would put things right? The Social Exclusion Unit made three key proposals [59].

1 Staying on in education
The predicted loss of unskilled jobs, and the lack of progression for those going straight into work at 16, meant that staying at school or in training until 18 was deemed a necessity, rather than the luxury it once had been. Reduction in poverty in the long term was seen to be dependent on raising the level of qualifications among young people and young adults in the bottom quarter of educational achievement. Crucial here was increasing the skill level of the 40 per cent of 16- to 18-year-olds with less than a Level 2 qualification.

2 Increased opportunities for young people
The goals to aspire to were higher standards of education for all, financial and other support for those who needed it most, and an end to a situation in which thousands of young people were not given the chance to make a better life for themselves and to make a bigger contribution to society.

3 A less fragmented pattern of services

The report also called for a single advice and support service that would work with schools and other universal services, offering targeted help to those with multiple or complex needs. Personal advisers would do one-to-one casework as well as working with specialist services and influencing the search for suitable work options.

developments in the past decade

Over the last ten years, progress has been made on all three fronts.

1 The 14 to 19 strategy

In March 2005, the government set out its strategy for education and training reforms in its 14-19 *Education and Skills* white paper. The strategy aims to ensure that all young people have opportunities to learn in a way that motivates and stretches them, and prepares them for adult life. The white paper included proposals to re-motivate disengaged learners, including extra support to master the basics, new curriculum choices and more choice over where and how to learn. The white paper also set out plans to pilot a programme for 14- to 16-year-olds based on the post-16 Entry to Employment programme (this has since evolved into the Key Stage 4 Engagement Programme – see Question 4).

2 Financial support

A number of initiatives have been implemented to support young people to continue in education or move on to training. These include cash allowances for young people from low-income families and towards the child-care expenses of young parents wanting to study, training schemes designed to equip young people with skills needed in the work place, and block grants to education authorities and Learning and Skills Councils to enable vulnerable young people to access good-quality education [44].

3 Every Child Matters: Change for Children

The government's Every Child Matters: Change for Children programme was introduced following the green paper *Every Child Matters* in 2003 and is underpinned by the Children Act 2004 [34]. It has set in train a major re-organisation of children's services. This includes a new duty on agencies to work together to deliver services to all children in their area and to meet clear targets for achieving good outcomes for children and families. The creation of Children's Trusts is seen as key to reducing service fragmentation. Responsible for the planning and delivery of local services for children, they lead the way in setting common targets across agencies and ensuring the pooling of budgets, which can help overcome barriers to joint work. Throughout this period, the work of Connexions (established in 2001) and the youth service have played a key role in tracking, working with and advocating for children aged 13 and over – in part helping to reduce service fragmentation.

the current position

The developments above are all reflected in the government's national strategy for reducing the number of young people who are NEET, which was published in 2008 [21]. The strategy links with plans to legislate (in the Education and Skills Bill) to raise the participation age so that by 2015 all young people stay in education or training until the end of the academic year in which they are 18. The strategy also links with the provisions for this vulnerable group of young people set out in the Children's Plan, which was published in December 2007.[4] And it builds on the recommendations of the Leitch Review of the UK's long-term skills needs, which stressed that it is necessary to get young people up to Level 2 qualifications by the age of 19 because that is the basic platform necessary for their being employable [25].

There are four key components to the government's NEET strategy:

- **Rigorous tracking** to identify early those young people who are NEET or at risk of becoming NEET. This will mean strengthening the tracking system by requiring all learning providers to notify the Connexions service as soon as any young person drops out, so that they receive immediate support. Information on the destination of former pupils will be passed on to schools to help them evaluate their information, advice and guidance (IAG) services.

- **Personalised guidance and support** to make sure young people know how to access education, training or employment and to enable them to overcome any barriers to their participation. The 'universal offer' for all young people is high-quality, comprehensive and impartial information, advice and guidance (IAG) to help young people make informed choices about their future. New national IAG quality standards are now in place, and local 14-19 prospectuses are available online in every area with up-to-date information about education and training options. By 2010 these prospectuses will be linked to a Common Application Process and Individual Learning Plan to support access to a diverse range of opportunities.

- **A full range of courses** so that young people no longer become NEET because they don't have the qualifications to move on or can't find the right provision. The reforms here include: help to catch up at Key Stage 3; new GCSEs, A-Levels and an extended

---

[4] The strategy also links with other recent and forthcoming initiatives arising from the Children's Plan: the Child Health Strategy, the Child and Adolescent Mental Health Services Review, the Youth Crime Action Plan and the Health and Social Care Strategy for young people in contact with the Youth Justice System. See www.dcsf.gov.uk/publications/childrensplan

project (ie, a single piece of work that requires planning, preparation, research and autonomous working, such as a report, a dissertation, a work of art or a design model, or a performance); a new Foundation Learning Tier (FLT), which will boost learning at Level 1, through skills for life work, vocational and subject-based learning, and personal and social development; new Diplomas in vocational studies; and more Apprenticeship places. These reforms are part of the government's 14 to 19 education and training reform programme. The NEET strategy aims to build more flexibility into the system so that the programme can be accessed throughout the year, not just in September.

• **Incentives to participation** is about finding ways to keep young people engaged and helping them re-engage quickly if they do drop out of learning or work. These include extending the scope of the financial incentives currently available and enabling young people to start a course during the academic year, rather than having to wait until the start of the next one. And from September 2008, the government is extending the September Guarantee – which guarantees the offer of a suitable learning place to all 16-year-olds leaving school – to all 17-year-olds.

and the future?

Our ambition remains that every young person, whatever their background, aspirations and aptitudes, is given the opportunity to progress through adolescence fully equipped to play an active role in society and gain the skills they need to enter the labour market. Together we can achieve this. [21]

This is a huge challenge, posed by the Secretary of State for Children, Schools and Families in his introduction to the NEET strategy described above.

There is already plenty in place to give hope that the strategy might succeed – not least the energy and enthusiasm of those implementing it at a local level, and the keen backing of colleagues at regional and national level. There is progress to improve outcomes for young people and their families by agencies working together to provide services in partnership, demonstrated by a strategic vision, shared responsibility and solutions agreed by senior officers across local authorities and primary care trusts – and with local areas having clear lines of accountability, through their Children's Trust and Local Strategic Partnership, to ensure that the contribution of all partners is monitored effectively.

Levers are in place, too. There is the Public Sector Agreement target to reduce the proportion of young people who are NEET by two percentage points by 2010. There are related indicators for specific sub-groups, such as increasing the participation of teenage mothers in education, employment or training to 60 per cent by 2010, and boosting the attainment and achievement of care leavers [24]. Furthermore, as part of the requirement on English local authorities to make spending decisions based on national targets and local priorities, and to agree these with central government, 115 of the 150 local authorities have chosen reducing the number of young people who are NEET as one of their top priorities. And the government's work with a small group of local authorities (NEET Hotspots) to support innovative work on issues identified in their local NEET improvement plan, is to be extended to a second wave of authorities later in 2008.[5]

All these are welcome developments, especially at a time of mounting concern about how fiendishly difficult it is to tackle the unequal life chances that confront one in ten of our young people. Education and training (increasingly referred to as learning and skills) are key elements of the drive to raise standards, widen participation, promote social inclusion and promote productivity [65]. But against this backcloth, we know, too, that some young people are consistently underperforming across key areas, and that social mobility has stalled. The life chances of our young people are now more strongly determined by their background and upbringing than for previous generations [48]. That is why attention to the needs of young people has to be so much broader than a narrow focus on their employment or education status. It should take account, too, of the importance of promoting more equal access to opportunities to develop the personal and social skills that will have a direct impact on their progress as they become adults.

---

[5] Phase 1 Hotspots are local authorities who won bids for up to £30,000 for this work. It was monitored by Government Offices, with feedback from local authorities to the Department for Children, Schools and Families. The Phase 2 programme is likely to follow a similar format.

how the review was conducted

The review aimed to focus on research studies conducted in the UK, supplemented by research from other countries (when available in English) that might offer useful insights and ideas for practice. We did not set a specific time-frame for studies as we were unsure of what might be available.

Policy and discussion documents and other non-research papers have also been scrutinised, either because they were mentioned in research studies or because their subject matter is relevant to the review. These include information from the analysis of longitudinal cohort studies and other national data; studies commissioned by government departments and reports from national inspection agencies; and small-scale research studies and local case-study material, the latter being a method commonly used by the non-formal learning sector to reflect professional opinion about interventions.

With both the research and other material the intention has been to draw on the views of those with expertise in the subject matter, notably professionals (those in practice and those involved in research, policy development and implementation) and family members (young people and their parents and other relatives). Academics, service providers and colleagues in practice and management posts in children's services helped devise the questions to explore. They also provided invaluable links to local projects and national programmes. All this has enabled us to draw on material from about a fifth of local administrative areas (local authorities or their equivalents), mainly in England, Scotland and Wales, but also in Northern Ireland and the Republic of Ireland.

This was a structured, rather than a systematic, review of evidence about young people who are NEET. Had we attempted a systematic review, studies that were of potential interest to readers because of their useful findings about attitudes or experiences would have been excluded because of weakness in their methodology. We were aware of the lack of investment in robust evaluation in some sectors working with young people, as acknowledged in the long-standing and lively debate about how to measure change in people's lives. In setting out to conduct a structured review, our aim has been to collect and analyse material from a wide variety of sources and then explore common themes.

Database and library searches were conducted for us by colleagues at The National Youth Agency, the National Foundation for Educational Research and the National Children's Bureau. This was followed by our own scrutiny of internet websites and databases by other organisations, including the British Library.

Comment is needed here about the nature of the evidence that we explored. The search terms EET and NEET, in long and shorthand, were not necessarily categories built into agency library systems or databases. Therefore, initial searches were followed by scrutiny of publications about the administrative or policy sub-groups of young people likely to be outside work or learning. The dilemma, as others have discovered before us [64], was where to start and when to stop. The policy agenda for this topic is far reaching. Some interventions (such as computer or literacy training) are designed with education, employment or training outcomes in mind, while others (such as mentoring or health advice) might have an impact on a young person's ability to access work or learning even though they were not designed with that particular outcome in mind.

And the review has not set out to provide a comprehensive mapping exercise of current programmes designed to increase young people's participation in work or learning or to reduce the risk of their becoming NEET. Rather we refer to some of the schemes we have learnt about and give links to other sources of information about interventions.

As a result, there will be gaps in what we have read and drawn on – about evaluations or research studies completed, about work in progress, about initiatives for particular sub-groups of young people who are NEET, and about local developments in policy and practice.

There are other considerations about the nature of the studies that we have drawn on.

First is the question of size. Some of the national studies have a very small sample. The local studies, by their very nature, cannot be taken as representative of the country as a whole. And cohort studies are likely to understate the problem since they rely on postal information and do not, for example, include young people in special schools or those who are outside mainstream provision because they are excluded from school or locked up in a custodial setting.

Second, there is the challenge of researching the lives and experiences of young people. There are difficulties in trying to track and evaluate the lives of young people who are busy negotiating the ups and downs of their life – a life that one project referred to as full of routes with 'dead ends, bridges, blind alleys and sudden gateways'. And it is hard to evaluate programmes if users tend to engage, drift off and dip back in again. Equally, there are difficulties in trying to measure progress beyond the life of a project or someone's involvement in it, or to judge whether change is sustained over time. Some follow-up studies do now exist, with either short-term review a few months after completion or a longer-term review after several years. More commonly, though, this has not been possible – as a result, some of the longitudinal studies we have included have interviewed different people at the start and end of a programme study.

Third, there is the question of what can and should be monitored and measured. There are very few studies about young people and education, employment or training – from the UK or elsewhere – that seek to measure in a robust way the change that different service responses make to young people's lives. In other words, there is a focus on process (what happens), rather than outcome (what changes). Both are important to aid the development of sound service responses to identified need.

And where outcomes are included in evaluations, there is debate about what sort of outcomes to consider. The debate is about the relative strengths of 'soft' and 'hard' outcomes, terms that some of those involved in youth or NEET work reject in favour of 'primary' or 'positional' change.

Primary (soft) outcomes are the changes in young people's skills, attitudes and capacity. The change is about becoming equipped with the personal and social skills to function well in life. If these are gained, young people will be better able to function independently, express themselves, engage in problem solving, transfer knowledge across situations and have positive relationships and pro-social attitudes. In turn, these gains may help bring about positional (hard) outcomes. These are changes to young people's position or life situation, such as re-engaging with school or securing a job or completing a training course. So while primary outcomes are about the benefits of participating in activity, positional outcomes are about how that impacts on later life.

Both sorts of outcomes present dilemmas for research.

Progress towards primary outcomes such as confidence and self-esteem can be hard to record and measure. Their evidential strength can be increased by collecting and comparing the perspectives of different participants – the greater the consensus between views, the more robust the evidence about the outcome achieved.

With positional outcomes, the problem is more about these being the preferred targets for funders and the tension that arises if that agenda dominates. When the main aim of workers is to engage and motivate young people, and to help stimulate the growth of personal autonomy and a 'mindset for learning', it can be hard for workers to find the time and enthusiasm for accurate recording of hard outcomes. On a more positive note, policy developments in the past decade mean that there is much more robust data collection and local area information available than at the time (1999) of the government's first report on this group of young people, and some national surveys conducted since then have drawn on much larger study samples.

The most relevant individual studies that we have relied on for messages about practice are described at the end of the review, immediately before the references. We hope that the detail there will help readers decide which particular texts might merit closer scrutiny for their own work. We have aimed to provide similar information about each study but this has not always been possible, so gaps remain here, too.

For all the reasons explored above, caution and an enquiring mind are needed when reading this review. Research does not provide us with definitive answers, and there is always the possibility that we are probing it with the wrong questions in mind. The review pulls out some topical issues for those working in and with children's services. We hope that readers raising queries that have not been addressed will decide to dip into the source material itself and discover more for themselves and their colleagues.

Questions explored for research and practice messages

question 1
Why do young people become and stay NEET, and how many young people are we talking about?

There is a lot of discussion in the literature about the circumstances that are likely to propel young people into NEET status and then make it difficult for them to move on into work or further learning. Most commentators sound caution about drawing firm conclusions, however. They point to the wide variety of young people's experiences and our current lack of knowledge about what is cause and what is consequence in this area.

The position has been summarised as follows – the pathway from education to work is less well defined than the path taken from school to the world of college and university, leaving some young people more disadvantaged than their peers. Young people who have personal or family problems to deal with are more likely to struggle at school, so the options of further education become closed to them. These problems are then compounded by non-engagement in work or learning, and so the cycle of social exclusion tightens and endures [31].

Within this broad framework, there are more specific factors that shape young people's options and influence their becoming or staying NEET. These have been described as relating to young people's personal and family circumstances, the 'system' in which they operate and the influence of providers of education and work opportunities. These factors are set out below [58].

young people-centred factors

- Poor educational engagement and attainment are linked to negative school experiences, truancy and exclusion in Year 11 especially, and low grades in GCSEs. It has been estimated that one in four young people aged 19 lack a basic qualification and that one in five of them lack the basic literacy and numeracy needed for today's world. The literacy level of more than half of young people and young adults between 16 and 25, and the numeracy level of three-quarters of them, are at or below Level 1 (the equivalent of GCSE grade D-F).

- A range of family difficulties can impact on young people's behaviour – poor relationships between children and adults, parental conflict and separation, loss and bereavement, undue caring responsibilities, and personal and social difficulties that lead to lack of confidence, self-esteem and aspirations [57].

- Learning to take and manage risks is part of every young person's development, but serious and inappropriate risk-taking behaviour can have an adverse impact on a young person's chances in life – including and leading to alcohol and drug misuse, antisocial and offending behaviour and homelessness, for example.
- Other circumstances, such as having a disability or special educational needs, mental health problems (in parents or the young person, or both), being in or on the edge of public care, belonging to a minority ethnic group or having refugee or asylum status, are all associated with young people either becoming or staying NEET.

system-centred factors

- Young people in communities affected by deprivation and intergenerational unemployment appear to be more likely to have a poor sense of mobility, suffer discrimination in the labour market, lack suitable role models and lack access to suitable jobs in their local area. There is differential access to work in rural, urban and suburban localities, and – generally – less chance of finding work in areas with a history of manufacturing or mining industry.
- Areas with poor transport infrastructure, and with poor and inadequate housing, are more likely to have a larger number of young people who are NEET, because young people are hampered from accessing further education and job opportunities.
- Other system factors include patchy knowledge about available options beyond school-leaving age, financial disincentives for young people to remain in education or training, and poor information about the financial support that might make a difference to young people's choices at 16.

provider-centred factors

- Providers of education, training or work can all influence the opportunities available for young people. They all have a role to play in helping young people see the long-term benefits of making wise choices at 16.
- Employers may have unrealistic expectations of young people fresh from school and their recruitment patterns may limit access by young people who are not on their established networks. Those interviewing young people may not have a clear enough grasp of how a vocational qualification equates with academic achievement.
- Lengthy application procedures for work or learning can act as a deterrent to young people impatient to move on quickly, just as a

lack of incentives can dent their enthusiasm to try out or stick with new opportunities. More understanding of why young people drop out of work or learning might generate ways of helping promote greater stability. Some common reasons are about not getting on with staff or employers, not liking the course or the work, pressure from family and peers, and finance and travel problems.

how many young people are we talking about?

Latest government statistics estimate that just under one in ten (9.4 per cent) of 16- to 18-year-olds in England were not in education, employment or training at the end of 2007 [23]. (This is, of course, a national average – there are significant variations at local level.)

The proportion of young people who are NEET has remained broadly similar throughout the past decade. (While there has been a decline over the last two years, this was from a peak reached at the end of 2005 [21, 23]). In 2007, this amounted to 189,000 young people – more than enough to fill London's new Wembley Stadium twice over [23]. In addition, the government's NEET strategy, published in 2008, indicates that almost a further quarter-million 16- to 18-year-olds (248,400) are in work that offers no training opportunity [21]; most of these are 18-year-olds.

Although the overall size of the group remains relatively stable, its composition varies considerably. It is estimated that only around one per cent of 16- to 18-year-olds are 'long-term NEET', defined as young people who are NEET at each of the three survey points at age 16, 17 and 18. Other young people are regularly moving in and out of NEET status. And in certain areas of the country, the percentage of young people who are NEET is higher than the national average – as it is for certain schools, or for young people from some minority ethnic groups or with particular vulnerabilities. The national statistics represent a snapshot of young people who are NEET at one particular time.

The NEET figures used by government for target and performance purposes combine administrative data on the number of young people participating in education and training with survey information to identify the activity of those not in education or training. These estimates are available for England only.

Local authority targets and performance, on the other hand, are monitored using information compiled and maintained in each local authority area by the Connexions service, which works with young people aged 13 to 19. The annual NEET statistic is the average percentage of the total number of young people recorded as not being in work, training or education at the end of November, December and January. This figure includes an adjustment, derived from a nationally used formula, for the small number of other young people in each area whose records are no longer current.

Despite the intensive activity that goes into tracking, counting and updating the number of young people who are NEET, the results are bound to be somewhat uncertain because young people are constantly moving in and out of the NEET group. Some young people not in education, employment or training are never recorded as NEET, some are recorded once only, others dip in and out throughout the year. But overall, there is cyclical variation – with a peak in the summer, when young people have left school or college but not yet taken up a work or other learning opportunity, followed by a marked fall in the autumn as they take up education and training opportunities.

Part of the answer to 'how many' young people are NEET is the question 'what counts as NEET?' In Scotland, the Scottish Executive estimates that there are 35,000 young people in this group – but when factors such as young people choosing to take time out after leaving school (as a gap year, doing voluntary work or travelling, and not claiming benefits) are taken into account, the number reduces to a core group of 20,000 who are NEET and in need of support to engage in work or learning. A survey of 18-year-olds in England and Wales found that only around 8 of the 14 per cent young people who are NEET deemed themselves as unemployed. Although the remainder were not in work or learning, they were engaged in some other activity – such as a gap year, voluntary work or caring for a child [23].

Categorisation

Young people who are NEET come with the same rich diversity that characterises all other young people of their age – they do not form one homogenous group. But agencies do tend to group them in some way, as a means of understanding the young people's circumstances and of developing services. This is generally done by administrative category (such as leaving care or having a disability), rather than by need (such as improved social skills or family relationships). The literature identifies the different ways in which agencies strive to cluster the young people into NEET sub-groups and we consider this categorisation in more detail later in the review.

It is helpful to try and think of young people in terms of their support needs. (Connexions staff assess young people as needing intensive, some or minimum support, depending on their individual needs.) We have adapted the following list of categories from the work of researchers exploring the literature for the Scottish Executive [64]. We use it to show one possible way of distinguishing the amount of help that might be needed. Another, more common, way of breaking down the group as a whole is used later, at Question 6.

As when using any clustering system, a sensitive approach is needed. The order below is not intended as a hierarchy. The groups are not mutually exclusive – a teenage mother could have 'elected' to be a mother as well as being economically 'inactive', for example. And it would be as unwise to slip into referring to young people by short-hand terms such as 'inactives' and 'residuals', as some argue it is to call young people 'NEETs'. We should also guard against any assumption that those who experience difficulties in their life have lower aspirations about their future than those who seem to make a smoother transition from school to work.

- **Elected NEET status** – so called because of choices made on leaving school, as explained above. Non-participation will be planned and/or unproblematic and the young people are highly likely to move on to further education or training or work at the end of their gap year. These young people may (but, arguably, should not) be included in research samples about young people's status as NEET.

- **Barely NEET status** – these are young people who, though currently classified as NEET, are well placed and well disposed to find work or training or education and so are likely to need minimal support to make that move. Some will be the young people who enter the NEET group once and then move on to a settled and secure destination. The reason for being NEET may be that they have completed a course, or chosen then decided against pursuing post-16 education, or have left or lost a job or a work-based training place.

- **Inactive NEET status** – this group consists of young people who, through choice or otherwise, are not in a position to take up a learning or work opportunity at present. For example, this could include young people who are teenage parents or have substantial other caring responsibilities at home (the latter are sometimes referred to as young carers), or who have an illness or disability that is so severe that work is not a viable option. Though not able at present to take up a work or learning opportunity, these young people still count as NEET for the purpose of NEET reduction targets, but are usually recorded as 'not available' or 'economically inactive'. It would also include the 3,000 or so young people under 18 who are held in custodial establishments. Their details are recorded separately on the Connexions database, and these records are held by the area in which their custodial establishment is located. Government policy is to exclude them from that area's NEET figures because they would have a disproportionate and misleading effect.

- **Residual NEET status** – this is the group that most studies focus on. They are the young people sometimes referred to by commentators as 'core NEETS', those who make up the 'churn' of repeated re-entry into NEET status. Some will have intermittent periods in low-paid and temporary work and short training courses. They may lack motivation and direction, but may respond well to short-term support and encouragement to engage or re-engage.

Others in this group are likely to need longer-term support to tackle and overcome the multiple barriers to their successful participation in learning or work. These are young people who stay NEET for longer periods of time or move in and out of NEET status repeatedly. They are the ones most at risk of future problems associated with social and economic exclusion – poor health, offending behaviour, mental health problems, substance misuse, poverty, poor housing, low wages and long-term unemployment. They are more likely to have social and behavioural problems themselves and to be described by some commentators as 'generational NEETs' in the sense of coming from families where adult unemployment is the accepted norm. They are the young people who need more intensive and long-term support to overcome their difficulties and engage with education, employment or training. They will often have had negative experiences of education and training and will have been away from it for some time.

For young people who have 'residual NEET status', it is not just a question of engaging or re-engaging them in activity. At least some of the risk factors that act in combination to leave them feeling disaffected may need to be addressed before the young person can engage seriously in a formal education or training programme. Some will be a long way from entering work or a structured environment – and they will need considerable support, encouragement and flexible provision if they are to leave the NEET group permanently. Focused help may succeed in nudging them in the right direction, taking small but important first steps along the way, rather than getting them quickly to where they might aspire to be.

question 2
How can formal education settings engage with the NEET to EET agenda?

There has long been debate about the role of formal education in children's development, including the influence that schools and colleges have on the choices young people make after compulsory schooling. Government reports have identified the school-based barriers to young people's educational achievement. A common complaint among disadvantaged young people is that the approach and attitude of many schools fails to harness and sustain their interest in education. There are three key areas to consider: what happens in school, the arrangements for education and training beyond 16, and the lack of financial support to continue in learning. Recent concerns have focused on the need for schools and colleges to work more collaboratively with other agencies, and for the improved participation of children, young people and families in decisions about education and services. All these developments have informed the government's strategy for increasing young people's opportunities to participate in education, employment and training.

what happens in school

Key research findings have suggested a number of problems arising from what happens in schools – the school curriculum is not flexible enough to motivate the range of pupils on its roll, insufficient account is taken of young people's different learning styles, teachers often lack the skills to deal with young people whose behaviour presents a challenge to staff, and there is a shortage of good-quality careers advice.

The exclusion and truancy that are consequent (in part, at least) on the above have an adverse impact on young people's life chances. Young people who truant persistently in Year 11 are eight times more likely than their peers to become NEET at 16. They are also more likely to end up in full-time work that is characterised by low pay, no training and no career advancement. Young people excluded in Year 10 or 11 are two to three times more likely to become NEET. Exclusion also has a disproportionate impact on certain groups of pupils, including boys, African-Caribbean young people, those in care and pupils with special educational needs.

More generally, the requirement to achieve imposed targets contributes to schools focusing disproportionately on young people who are likely to achieve and on academic rather than vocational qualifications. This focus serves to marginalise or set aside the interests of those young people who feel they will not succeed or who believe that qualifications are irrelevant to success. These young people's feelings are then compounded by gaps in pastoral support and their sense of being ignored and misunderstood.

options after school

Here, too, there has been consensus about the difficulties that can contribute to young people not engaging in work or further learning. The sudden break in routine as young people leave school can be difficult to adjust to. The lack of opportunity to 'dip back' into school if other options fail and the confusing proliferation of courses for post-16 qualifications can contribute to a failure to engage. And particular problems are associated with some options: work-based training is characterised by short courses and a high drop-out rate; insufficient resources are available to support particularly vulnerable young people through college; and approval for in-work training can be difficult to secure and the training itself hard to commit to.

The lack of financial support can be a particular problem. Young people and their families often face an uphill struggle to support learning beyond 16. Many give up, defeated by the complexity and inflexibility of the benefit system, the inordinate cost of travel to participate in learning or work opportunities, and the prospect of mounting debt that stretches well into the future.

messages about promising approaches

The powerful influence of formal education on young people's life chances has long been a recurrent and prominent feature in the literature. Some of the key messages are set out below.

A resource in adversity School can be a key protective and preventive resource for children experiencing social adversity. It can have a positive and long-lasting effect on their social as well as educational development. It can serve as a buffer for some children against some of the worst effects of socioeconomic disadvantage. The normality, routine and safety that school provides may be powerfully therapeutic for vulnerable young people, and key teaching and other staff may act as catalysts in children's lives [2]. These messages are not new – the evidence to support them dates back almost three decades and has been repeated many times since.

A learning school A more recent message relates to the style in which schools operate. A study (for the Department for Children, Schools and Families) of mixed-heritage pupils in six areas points to the need to create learning schools that are 'outward looking, open to new ideas and constantly adapt to the changing ethnic composition and needs of the local community'. The key ingredients for a successful learning school include:

- a leadership that is keen to understand and anticipate the implications of new policies at national and local level
- the ability to collect and analyse achievement data and disseminate conclusions to the school community
- staff who are prepared to challenge their own assumptions and stereotypes of pupil and family aspirations and abilities

- the active encouragement of innovation by staff in a blame-free environment
- being open to the ideas and views of parents – and being prepared to provide parents with learning opportunities to assist them in meeting their child's educational needs [60].

Part of this is about providing young people and those close to them with information about the maze of vocational courses on offer, the value of qualifications that attach to each, and how to navigate applications and financial support. Teaching staff can also help by knowing and talking about the world of work. Pupils may have very little understanding of jobs available, and unrealistic expectations of the job market. They may not realise what skills are needed by employers, or even recognise that they have them. They may also sometimes need help to counter the negative views of peers and families [43].

Children's learning Recent analysis of longitudinal data about cognitive and non-cognitive skills adds weight to the importance to be attached to both the manner and content of children's learning in school. Children displaying the domains of 'writing off (being dismissive of) adults and adult standards', and 'inconsequential behaviour' (for example, misbehaviour in class) were significantly less likely than their peers to stay at school beyond 16. The researchers recommend that schools place more emphasis on delivering social skills training, responding to children's depression, and finding ways of boosting parental interest in their children's learning [9].

Assessing and addressing special needs The government's recent Bercow Review [6], which explored children's speech and language skills, points to the risks of leaving needs unattended: lower educational attainment, behavioural problems, emotional and psychological difficulties, poorer employment prospects, challenges to mental health and, in some cases, a descent into criminality. Among the research referred to is a survey in 2005 of 200 young people in an inner-city secondary school, which found that 75 per cent of the pupils had communication difficulties that hampered relationships, behaviour and learning. The incidence of other special educational needs is also well documented – with disproportionate numbers of young people who are NEET having dyslexia, dyspraxia and/or dyscalculia, which may or may not be diagnosed and supported in school and college. The challenge here is for early attention. This means assessment, both at a young age and as soon as a possible difficulty comes to light, followed by appropriate support or treatment.

Teaching skills for youth workers College tutors may not always be the right teachers for this particular group of young people. But the youth and community workers who are confident and competent about engaging with them may not feel equipped to deliver the skills training needed, especially numeracy, literacy and language. Workers need to know what training is available and how to judge its quality, and how to access it [46].

Informal activities outside the school day The organisation of on-site leisure opportunities via extended schools is particularly important for those young people at the lower age range who cannot access off-site peer group activities themselves. If teachers are involved, such activities can offer young people the benefit of seeing teachers more as 'an authority' in a subject, as opposed to being seen as people who are 'in authority'. It is argued that this shift in perception can help improve young people's engagement in formal learning [63].

NEET prevention work

The value of early prevention is a common thread in the literature about the school careers of young people who are NEET. The clear message is that if the right help is available early on, it offers a far greater prospect of ensuring EET status than trying to shift entrenched and negative attitudes further down the line. This is about timely intervention before disengagement and disaffection set in – to deal with problems such as bullying and racism at an early stage, and to help schools forge relationships with (and between) families and communities, not only for the sake of current pupils but also in the hope of having a positive impact on their younger siblings.

The messages below are all highlighted in the literature.

Alternative curriculum Offering an alternative curriculum appears to be essential in engaging young people at risk of disengaging from learning. The traditional academic pathway does not suit everyone and can lead to disengagement from education altogether. An alternative curriculum is likely to prevent some young people from dropping out of school and to prepare them for further education and/or training with a vocational element.

Transition Continued support at key stages of transition, especially as children move on from primary and then secondary school, can help ensure that those with intensive support needs are helped to negotiate experiences that can, all too easily, shake confidence and motivation and heighten the risk of disengagement and disaffection. The other key transition point is when young people move back to school from a less formal setting. Circumstances can change dramatically – and fast. It is particularly important to ensure that support is in place to help young people guard against slipping back into behaviour patterns that may have caused, or contributed to, their removal in the first place [65].

Listening It is important to listen to young people, to take their views seriously and to respond in practical ways to what they say. In one local study of young people who were NEET, almost half said they would have benefited from more flexible education while at school – and over half said that help with personal problems while at school (or since leaving) might have prevented their becoming NEET. Young people cited better financial help, better advice about options and more help with job searching as useful in preventing their dropping out of work or learning opportunities. Most young people faced multiple barriers to moving into EET status, including lack of basic skills and qualifications, personal problems, lack of job application and interview experience, poor motivation, their offending behaviour, a lack of suitable work or learning opportunities and limitations imposed by poor transport provision [33].

Supporting young people to make decisions It is important to support young people to make decisions about their future, especially if they lack this support at home or feel they are not listened to at school because of their poor behaviour and attainment. Young people are less likely to become NEET if they feel confident in themselves, have a sense of achievement and self-worth and have aspirations about their future. Participating in school or college life, such as through school councils or interviewing for new staff, seem to be promising approaches in helping support young people to make choices that will have a positive impact on their life chances [8]. The extension of the healthy school initiative into colleges of further education might prove to be another development that helps young people make informed and positive decisions about their lifestyle [10].

Working with and mitigating negative attitudes Negative attitudes towards school, in which education and qualifications are seen as having little value in the world of work, seem to contribute to young people becoming NEET [56]. Such attitudes can arise from boredom, poor relationships with teachers or an anti-school ethos. These may then be compounded by, or cause, other school-related problems, such as poor attendance and attainment [12, 58]. So in designing interventions, it is important that schools and colleges understand the characteristics of young people who are at risk of becoming NEET. Successful interventions recognise the needs of individual pupils and offer appropriate levels of support.

Question 2 - Summary points

- Historically, disadvantaged young people have long complained that schools fail to engage or motivate them – the curriculum has not been flexible, and little account has been taken of their preferred learning styles. Many have been marginalised by a disproportionate focus on academic rather than vocational qualifications – a focus that has been influenced by external government targets.

- Schools and other formal education providers have a key role to play in securing engagement in learning. The literature highlights the importance of offering an alternative curriculum, providing support at key stages of transition, enabling holistic support from a range of agencies, listening to (and acting on) the views of young people and securing the active involvement of parents. Offering on-site informal activities outside the school day may help younger students in particular to engage with formal learning.

- Young people who are not following traditional academic routes can find the maze of possible pathways ahead hard to navigate. They need help to understand and negotiate vocational routes – otherwise many give up, defeated by the cost of travel to participate, the prospect of mounting debt and the complexity and inflexibility of the benefits system.

- Many young people have limited understanding of the world of work. Schools have an important role to play in helping them understand how the job market works and what skills are needed by employers.

question 3
What does non-formal learning have to offer?

In recent years several national and local studies have explored the concept of non-formal learning for young people who are NEET or likely to become so. This has been in the wake of the government's intention to make progress beyond academic achievement alone. Alongside a demanding standard for formal qualifications to be achieved by age 19, it has aimed to promote 'other achievements in key skills and the community' [59]. This is non-formal learning.

The term non-formal learning is broadly understood to mean the sports, leisure, arts projects and other recreational activities that are carried out predominantly through youth work approaches [50] [see box on page 57-58]. Non-formal learning take place in a range of settings, including schools, community and youth centres, sports clubs and art venues, and may be provided by statutory, voluntary, community or private sector organisations. Other terms are used interchangeably – especially 'informal' rather than 'non-formal' and 'education' rather than 'learning'. But in essence, what we are talking about is activity that doesn't count as formal qualifications.

The experiences of many thousands of young people are described in a wide range of recent studies[6]. They cover the following topics:

- ways of promoting young people's learning and development through non-formal activities and relationships, and how local services can operate flexibly but within a national framework [50]

- work by community organisations to re-engage 13- to 19-year-olds who are disaffected with school, work or training and either disengaged or at risk of dropping out [1]

- young people's views on the opportunities provided by organised, out-of-school activities for the development of social skills and on the impact of those opportunities on their attitudes and behaviour in school [63]

- the use of sport and other leisure activities as a basis for establishing relationships with young people alienated from mainstream agencies and authority figures – and then, through discussion with responsible adults, helping to influence young people's behaviour by widening their horizons and helping them access new learning or work opportunities [16]

- an action research programme in eight areas to explore whether non-formal Awards (like the Duke of Edinburgh scheme) are a useful way for pre-employment programmes to deliver personal and social development skills, such as self-confidence, self-esteem and group working [38]

[6] There is a short description of most of these studies at the end of this review, immediately before the references section.

- action research to identify the key success elements in practice – and to develop appropriate resources – to help develop young people's literacy, language and numeracy skills [46].

Also relevant is a somewhat different exercise – the analysis of longitudinal data about children's early cognitive and non-cognitive skills [9]. This study is relevant here because of what it shows us about the importance of non-cognitive (or soft) skills, ie the ones that are the main focus of non-formal learning.

messages from the studies

What overall conclusions can be drawn from this rather disparate group of studies?

First, it's important to acknowledge what these studies cannot tell us. They don't reveal much about which aspects of non-formal learning make the difference – nor can we say much about how, or indeed whether, changes endure in the long term. Nevertheless, there are important messages for practice that can be drawn out – in particular, about the types of provision that young people find attractive or acceptable. These messages are described briefly below. Among other things, they cover the aspects of a service that are important to service users – these relate to venue, style of delivery and the attitudes of workers.

Venue and focus A range of venues are acceptable to young people – including home, school and local community locations. Young people are likely to feel more at ease in settings that provide universal services rather than feeling they are being singled out or targeted as being different, vulnerable or needy. The range of activities should be broad and offer choices. Sport is not right for everyone, for example. The focus should be on fun and offering something that is different from what happens during the school day, even if provided on school premises. The emphasis should be on 'things to do' rather than 'services to access'. A mix of one-to-one learning and group activity is helpful, with a flexible delivery style that includes outreach work, a single base for accessing provision and evening and weekend activities.

Active participation Young people also value the chance to contribute to activities, rather than just be the recipients of services – for example, being able to bring relatives or friends to a project, or passing on the skills they have gained to newer participants. They also value having their competence acknowledged, through certificates or progress to a higher level of involvement. Structure is accepted, indeed welcomed, as is the chance to get involved in activities gradually so that young people can ease out of their comfort zone and take small steps forward at their own pace.

Autonomy (agency) A crucial gain for young people from non-formal learning is thought to be an improved sense of autonomy or agency. This allows young people to feel they are gaining control over their life, rather than feeling they are a victim of fate or vulnerable to changes in circumstances beyond their control. Education is about learning 'from the inside' what it is to lead a fulfilling life; having confidence in social interaction, gained through taking responsibility while involved in activities; having a sense of belief in oneself, despite the odds and past experiences; and taking decisions, both for oneself and on behalf of others.

Multiple gains The gains outlined above can also have a wider impact on other areas of young people's lives. Success breeds confidence that can be a spur to success in other areas of life. Examples in the literature include the increased self-confidence that can help reduce the chance of young people engaging in over-risky behaviour and the higher locus of control that can lead to better health outcomes. The self-awareness and other types of knowledge gained can enhance the ability of young people to make informed choices in life. This knock-on effect includes the potential for improving formal learning, as skills and knowledge are transferred to other settings. Examples of this include the ability to speak out with greater confidence and to do so in a more pro-social way (for example, by answering back less in class).

Influential adults A number of adults have key roles to play in the success of non-formal learning. Adults involved directly in non-formal learning place prime importance on making a specific and conscious effort to work with young people in ways that highlight their wider life options, helping them to make the link between what they are doing now and what they could choose to do next. These are the values of youth work, of those skilled at working with young people on the edge. Consistent and positive relationships are considered key to promoting a disposition in young people to other forms of learning besides non-formal. Adults assume a range of different tasks – they provide expertise but also act as role model, leader, fellow learner, bridge, facilitator, mentor, mediator and motivator. Other adults have an equally influential role to play – for example, local ownership of non-formal learning programmes is dependent on acceptance by respected adults in the young people's community.

Parallel work The literature points to the importance of non-formal learning programmes including parallel work on those issues that might otherwise prevent young people from taking up work or training opportunities. These include accommodation difficulties, benefit and other income issues, fraught relationships with parents, and the needs arising from young people having parenting or other caring responsibilities. There are also clear messages from practice about the value of trying to counter negative experiences of education through work to assess and treat dyslexia and other specific learning difficulties (albeit that these should, in an ideal world, have been tackled much earlier in the young person's life).

Enduring difficulties It is important to be realistic about enduring difficulties. While much can and is being done to influence young people's life chances through non-formal learning, practitioners need to remain realistic about what they can achieve. In particular, they need to help young people reach some sort of equilibrium between desired and realistic outcomes. There are external and systemic barriers that create unequal access – for example, financial barriers, transport, the threshold for services, and the level and nature of local funding for projects. Internal barriers to progress can be deep rooted and will need different timescales to overcome. These are about things mentioned already – especially individual and family expectations and the negative educational experiences of children and parents. People use cover stories about their circumstances as a way of deflecting stigma and discrimination, so those involved in non-formal learning need to be particularly alert to ways of helping young people create and develop their life story.

Question 3 - Summary points

- Taking part in informal activities can boost young people's self-confidence and have a knock-on effect in other areas of their life – for example, leading to a reduction in inappropriate risk taking, the adoption of a more healthy lifestyle and an enhanced ability to make informed choices in relation to learning and training.

- Young people are more likely to be attracted to activities and informal learning programmes that are provided from universal and community-based settings, where the emphasis is on things to do rather than the provision of a service. The range of activities on offer should be broad, with lots of choice – and a mix of one-to-one learning and group activities.

- It is important for non-formal programmes to find ways to offer young people parallel support with everyday problems that can prevent them taking up learning and training opportunities – such as accommodation difficulties, benefit and income-related problems, family relationships and any parenting or caring duties.

- A flexible style of delivery is important – ideally, this should include outreach work and a single base for accessing provision and evening and weekend activities. Staff should be willing to work unsocial hours to fit in with young people's needs and lifestyles, be prepared to learn about young people's complex needs and be able to work with and alongside families.

- Forming consistent and positive relationships with influential adults leading informal activities can be a key factor in helping young people to engage in more formal learning. Adults need to be able to adopt a number of different roles – mentor, motivator, fellow learner and facilitator.

question 4
How effective are financial and work-based incentives designed to help young people stay in or return to learning or work?

All work designed to engage with young people will aim to inspire or enthuse them – few would doubt the desirability of such an approach and much has been written about the principles and practice approaches that are likely to achieve this aim. Our focus here is more specific, however – it is the financial and other hooks that are used as incentives to draw young people into education, employment and training. These hooks consist of both national programmes and pilots, and projects developed at a local level.

The government's 2004 report on social exclusion [52] identified two key components of successful work with young people who are NEET. One is advice and support from skilled professionals – the other is financial incentive. In answering Question 4, we consider the evidence relating to some of the financial support available to young people and, where appropriate, their families. (For the most part, incentives for others – employers, providers and local authorities – are dealt with under Question 5. However, the evidence relating to some financial incentives to support young people – for employers through Learning Agreements, and for learning providers through Entry to Employment (E2E) programmes – are discussed here.)

Education Maintenance Allowance (EMA) – cash help to stay in education between 16 and 18

The Education Maintenance Allowance (EMA) was piloted in a number of areas from 1999 and rolled out nationally for 16-year-olds from 2004. It aims to provide young people from families on a low income with help to meet the costs of staying in education beyond age 16. The intention is that a weekly cash payment will provide an incentive for young people to complete Years 12 to 14 at school or college and so ensure that financial circumstances are not a barrier to participation.

To qualify for the allowance, which is worth £10, £20 or £30 a week (depending on household income), young people must attend at least 12 hours per week of taught sessions that lead to a recognised qualification. The learner signs an EMA contract with the school, college or provider, and payments depend on the learner keeping to the contract. As an incentive throughout the whole period, the young person also receives a bonus payment for achievement.

Does it work?
On the positive side, the EMA has succeeded in preventing some young people from becoming NEET straight from school [65].

Evaluation of a pilot programme (in ten local areas in England from 1999) to see how different ways of making cash payments might impact on participation and achievement, showed a four per cent increase in participation in Year 12 and a six per cent increase in Year 13, both with good levels of retention during the year. The Scottish pilot project was more promising – participation rates increased by seven per cent overall and by nine per cent among pupils in the lowest income group [64].

However, the gains from the national programme in England that was rolled out from 2004 were more modest than the pilot. Continued participation at school or college at age 16 increased by only one per cent, rather than the expected four per cent. And by the time young people reached age 19, the programme had ceased to have a noticeable effect on participation levels in full-time education, and had no significant effect on attainment levels either.

But the programme did succeed in reducing the number of 16 and 17-year-olds taking up work with no training element – a route that is strongly associated with high levels of job turnover and young people becoming (and remaining) disengaged from learning and work.

The EMA programme has been less successful in attracting back into full-time education those young people who were already NEET, however. And there is evidence that its extension to young people joining a work-based learning programme (such as E2E, a pre-entry programme for those not ready to take up an apprenticeship) had an adverse impact on recruitment to those programmes. This was largely attributed to the EMA being means-tested (based on parental annual income), unlike the flat-rate training allowance that was previously available for this group. (It should be noted, however, that from June 2008 all E2E participants are now eligible for the full rate of EMA, regardless of household income.)

Other drawbacks to the scheme have been highlighted. One is the delay in payment being authorised. For this vulnerable group of young people, such delays can quickly lead to disillusionment and an increased risk of longer-term disengagement [33]. Overall, some commentators have deemed the EMA to have been over-sold as an instrument for improving participation – and especially as one for boosting attainment [58].

Care to Learn

Care to Learn provides financial support for teenage parents who want to continue in or return to learning. It pays up to £160 a week (£175 in London) to help with the cost of registered child care and travel. Support is available to any young parent who is under 20 on the day the learning starts, which can take place at a school, 6th form, FE college (or any other learning provider that receives public funding) or with a work-based learning provider (eg, an Apprenticeship with nonemployed status or an Entry to Employment programme). Entitlement is not dependent on a minimum number of hours – a young parent can choose to undertake part- or full-time learning, for anything from a few weeks to more than two years.

Does it work?

As part of the national evaluation of Care to Learn, four research reports commissioned by the Learning Skills Council were published in December 2007. All were based on qualitative research with relatively small numbers and were based largely on the perceptions of those involved with the programme. One report tracked the destinations of young parents who had been funded through Care to Learn in 2003-04 [17]. Just over half (52 per cent) the participants reported that they had completed their course during the academic year, while 7 per cent were still studying on the same course; 40 per cent said they had dropped out, however. More than four out of five (82 per cent) young parents said they would not have gone on a course if the programme had not paid for their child care.

A second report, a study of flexible provision for young mothers, emphasised the importance of providing a holistic approach to learning – one that addresses the broader context of their lives and helps them deal with a range of personal and practical problems [18]. The curriculum needs to relate to the learners' position as young mothers, embedding literacy and numeracy in everyday activities. It also needs to be varied and flexible enough to evolve depending on the characteristics of each group. The study also highlights the importance of accredited learning – many of the mothers had not done well at school and had never achieved qualifications, so accreditation gave them confidence and showed them they could use their learning to move on. Not surprisingly, the free on-site child care was seen as key to young mothers participating in learning.

Activity Agreements – financial support to re-engage

Activity Agreement pilots were launched in eight areas of England in April 2006 with the aim of re-engaging 16 and 17-year-olds who had been long-term NEET (ie, for 20 weeks or more). In return for agreeing to take part in tailored activities designed to help them progress towards a positive employment, education or training outcome, young people receive a weekly allowance of between £20 and £30. (The pilots were designed to test three variants: a weekly incentive of £20 for the young person; £30 per week for the young person; or £20 for the young person, plus £30 support for the family.) The agreement itself is a personally negotiated contract between a Connexions personal adviser and the young person, setting out specific steps that should be taken to help the young person move into education, training or employment (preferably with learning).

In its NEET strategy early in 2008, the government announced plans to extend Activity Agreement pilots to examine the effectiveness of engaging young people in an agreement as soon as they drop out of learning, rather than after 20 weeks of being NEET [21].

Do they work?

While it is early days, evaluation at the end of year one suggests that Activity Agreements were generally functioning well [47]. It was reported that many young people (up to 50 per cent) had left the programme early, mainly to enter some form of education, employment or training – suggesting that many young people are able to progress to some form of EET after relatively short periods of support. The financial allowance was felt to have been a useful hook to attract young people initially, although parents were more ambivalent about its value. But the combination of intensive support provided by personal advisers and a personalised, bespoke programme was thought to have played a key role in sustaining participation. A small qualitative study based on interviews with 37 young people (32 who had signed up to an Activity Agreement, and five who had declined) found that young people's reasons for signing up tended to be complex and multifaceted, but were generally underpinned by the financial incentive [39].

In most cases, pilots had failed to engage with some of the 'hardest to reach' young people, however, especially those estranged from their parents and living independently – this was attributed to a conflict of interest between benefit receipt and taking up the financial incentive of an Activity Agreement. The requirement to have been NEET for at least 20 weeks was also found to have significantly reduced the eligible population for the scheme [47].

Interestingly, while Activity Agreement pilots engaged in a wide range of marketing and publicity activity, the most effective strategies for entry to the scheme appear to have been the one-to-one engagement between personal advisers and young people themselves, and a 'word-of-mouth' increase in awareness among young people.

Learning Agreements

Learning Agreement pilots were also launched in eight areas of England in April 2006. (Four areas piloted both Learning Agreements and Activity Agreements; each initiative was also piloted separately in four other areas.) Learning Agreements are aimed at 16 and 17-year-olds in jobs without training. Under a Learning Agreement, young people take part in agreed activities, which must include undertaking a designated course. In some of the pilot areas, young people receive a monetary bonus if they are successful – and in two areas, employers receive subsidies to release young people to attend training sessions. In three pilot areas, neither the young person nor their employer receives any financial incentive.

Do they work?

An evaluation report at the end of the first year of Learning Agreement pilots found it was too early to report on outcomes [47]. Learning Agreements, which are delivered locally by Connexions and local Learning and Skills Councils, had generally been welcomed as a means of engaging with young people and their employers, but take-up rates were significantly lower than expected. Difficulties were reported in recruiting and retaining staff who could work effectively with both young people and employers – and who were able to 'sell' the initiative to employers. Learning Agreement take-up rates were found to be highest in areas where provision was dominated by key skills, basic skills and Technical Certificate programmes – in other words, where young people were largely recruited to provision that had been set up before their entry to the programme.

A small qualitative study involving interviews with young people who had signed up to Learning Agreements in pilot areas where no financial incentive was offered found that most signers had been motivated by improving their job prospects. They wanted to progress within their current job or move to an area of work that interested them more. An important reason for signing the Learning Agreement was that it was 'different from school' [40].

Entry to Employment (E2E) – cash bonus for pre-employment programme providers

The Entry to Employment (E2E) programme offers an incentive not only to learners (participants are eligible to claim Education Maintenance Allowance) but also a financial incentive to providers. Some learning providers can claim a qualification bonus when a young person achieves a Level 1 or equivalent qualification. The bonus is now paid at a basic or enhanced level, each linked to certain qualifications.

The E2E programme was launched in England in 2003 for young people aged 16 to 18 who are not participating in any form of post-16 learning. The scheme was introduced as the 'root of the apprentice tree' since it aims to enable young people to progress to an Apprenticeship, further vocational learning or employment. E2E targets young people who are not ready for more intensive work training. It is designed to help them develop their motivation and confidence, personal effectiveness and basic skills, and also to acquire vocational knowledge and skills, with opportunities to dip into a range of work and learning experiences in order to improve their readiness for employment. E2E is tailored to individual needs and an Individual Activity Plan is developed for every learner as the key to ensuring that they have a positive and flexible programme [58]. Learners on E2E programmes can apply for an Education Maintenance Allowance (EMA) – and from June 2008, all eligible learners are able to access the maximum EMA payment, regardless of household income.

Does it work?

On the question of financial incentive for providers, a study of non-formal Awards found that eligibility for the initial qualifications bonus was useful in engaging providers to use the Awards for providing the personal and social development aspects of training. However, it was not the driving force behind providers' decisions to make use of the Awards programmes [38].

On the effectiveness of E2E more generally, a survey in 2005 found a mixed picture. Overall, the scheme was considered effective in supporting the learning of personal and social skills – and the best programmes succeeded in responding well to young people's specific needs. Relatively few young people (only 6 per cent of those surveyed) went on to an apprenticeship, but a third moved on to a job or college place or work-based training. In the survey sample there was a good rate of progression for young people with disabilities (33 per cent), with a slightly lower rate achieved for those from minority ethnic groups (28 per cent) [58].

Downsides were reported, however. There were too few choices available in the vocational element of E2E, including only limited work experience opportunities. The survey also reported a shortage of suitable progression routes in terms of jobs or courses for those who have completed E2E, with some individual programmes being too fragmented to offer clear progression for the learners following them. Their poor experiences at school leaves them questioning the value of a series of courses unless those will clearly help them get a job.

The rapid intake to the scheme also caused problems with over-subscription. A shortage of resources to meet demand led to disappointment and de-motivation among some agencies and staff, and among young people in the hardest-to-reach groups, as some providers restricted eligibility to those most likely to complete the course. In addition, the programme replaced some much-needed pre-E2E provision, such as basic life skills, leaving a gap for some young people in need of the most intensive support.

Other complaints were that by allocating equal numbers of places around the country, the national programme failed to take different local authority needs into acccount, and that there was no provision for young people with additional needs – a particular problem because 16 and 17-year-olds are often considered too old for support from children's services, but too young for adult services.

Apprenticeships

An Apprenticeship is a structured programme of training that gives a young person the opportunity to work for an employer, learn on the job, build up knowledge and transferable skills, and gain nationally recognised qualifications in key skills, including National Vocational Qualifications (NVQs) [58]. While Apprenticeships are in part driven by meeting the skills needs of local employers, providing Apprenticeship places for young people is a key government priority for ensuring that more 16- to 19-year-olds are participating in post-compulsory education [20].

Over-16s used to apply for one of two schemes: the Foundation Modern Apprenticeship, equivalent to Level 2 ability, or the Advanced Modern Apprenticeship, pitched at Level 3 ability. However, these are now referred to simply as the Apprenticeship. (There is also a scheme for under-16s – the Young Apprenticeship.) All young people are offered training on the job and the chance to earn technical certificates, National Vocational Qualifications (NVQs) and qualifications in key skills [58].

In the year ending April 2006, just over a quarter of a million young people were engaged in an Apprenticeship, through one of 180 schemes operating across England in more than 80 sectors of industry [65]. In 2007, the House of Lords Select Committee on Economic Affairs called for the scheme to be expanded and overhauled [37].

Do they work?

Apprenticeships had a shaky start, as evidenced in a report from the Training Standards Council in 2000 [61]. The Council was critical that the Modern Apprenticeship had led to relatively low levels of retention and certification and that young people participated in some sectors, such as construction and engineering, for less time than was anticipated or needed. They also pointed to inadequate assessment of the basic and key skills young people needed to have under their belt before they joined a scheme, and to an unhelpful gap between what was being taught on site and off site.

But by the time of a Social Exclusion Unit report in 2004, they were generally seen to be a success. Employers valued Apprenticeships for the training they provided in intermediate skills and the scheme was extended to young people under 16, as mentioned above. Entitlement also became universal rather than selective [52].

Research studies have focused on age, completion rates and progress afterwards. Age did not seem to have an impact on completion rates, and non-completion did not have a significant impact on a young person's career progression or ability to find work. The quality and work of training providers was found to be a key influence on completion rates. However, no conclusions were drawn about whether even temporary support through the programme is helpful to young people in the future, or whether the ones who start and give up would have succeeded anyway. Concern is expressed about insufficient funding for the programme and about incentives being focused more on starting rather than completing the course [64].

Key Stage 4 Engagement Programme

Based on Entry to Employment for the over-16s, the Key Stage 4 Engagement Programme is a pilot programme, for 14- to 16-year-olds most at risk of disengagement. It is a personalised programme that comprises each learner's whole Key Stage 4 programme, with an emphasis on the development of personal, social and functional skills. The programme includes a work-focused component (preferably taking place in a work environment) and is underpinned by high-quality and regular support, advice and guidance from a trusted adult.

The national programme was piloted by 21 partnerships in 2006-07 and in 2007-08 ran in 71 partnerships across the country. From September 2008, the programme will expand to 101 pilots, providing 21,500 learner places across the country. The programme is based on a template devised by the Qualifications and Curriculum Authority (QCA), which builds on good practice and sets out clear principles. (These include that there should be clear progression routes identified for each young person and transitional support provided as they progress out of the programme.) However, it is up to individual partnerships to devise personalised programmes that meet the needs of learners and are appropriate to the local employment situation. An evaluation of the programme started in January 2007.

New Deal for Young People (NDYP) – intensive support for those claiming Jobseeker's Allowance

The New Deal for Young People aims to help 18- to 24-year-olds who have been in receipt of Jobseeker's Allowance for more than six months to get a job or train, learn and undertake work experience. The scheme is relevant to some young people who are NEET, because eligibility starts from age 18. Also, new proposals provide for this age group to be fast-tracked to help. Strictly speaking, the scheme does not provide young people with a financial incentive because there is no option not to take it up – benefit is withdrawn in the case of refusal. So we cover this later, under Question 8, about lessons that can be learnt from help given to adults.

financial incentives from non-government agencies

A new report from the voluntary agency Kids Company [29] describes its policy of giving young people weekly financial support, if needed as a supplement or in lieu of statutory benefits. It does so to deter young people from getting involved in criminal activity (such as theft, drug dealing and prostitution) because they have too little or no money from anywhere else. The allowances are payable for attending the organisation's Urban Academy, a centre where staff provide vulnerable young people aged 16 plus with therapeutic and social work interventions as well as educational opportunities. The section of the report on this aspect of the work suggests, from an analysis of the files of 240 young people receiving intensive support, that four-fifths of them succeeded in achieving an EET-related outcome. This included returning to education (34 per cent), returning to education and getting work (22 per cent), remaining in education (17 per cent), and getting work (8 per cent). The evaluation doesn't explore the association between success and receipt of an allowance, but does give a strong message about the high value attached to them and their impact on young people's sense of security and motivation.

case example

A cautionary tale – look behind the statistics
A young person was sacked from a training scheme that had been set up to recruit disaffected 16 and 17-year-olds to placements offering basic skills training and work experience, with a view to their then progressing to work-based training or employment.

Most young people joined the scheme when they tried to claim unemployment benefit. They were discouraged from claiming the benefit in favour of joining the scheme and getting a £45 per week training allowance. The expectation was that they would join the scheme because they fitted the criteria of being disadvantaged.

When the young person was sacked after 13 weeks in placement, he was told that in a month's time he could have a place at a mainstream job club, run by the same training provider. But his allowance would drop to £20 per week.

He was not officially recorded as having been dismissed. Rather, the change was recorded as an outcome of positive progression, implying that his problem had been solved by his participating in the first scheme. He was left feeling disillusioned, and with less cash in his pocket.

In the words of the researcher, the scheme 'hit the target but missed the point'.
[13]

Question 4 - Summary points

- The evidence suggests young people respond well to hooks and incentives – especially financial ones. For some young people, financial incentives are key to their successful engagement. Nevertheless, it can be an ongoing challenge to sustain their interest once they are on board. And the tension between a young person's learning and keeping the rest of their life going is a difficult one to resolve. It is all the more difficult for young people whose circumstances render them more vulnerable than their peers.

- It is important to consider how best to incentivise those young people who live apart from their family. They may well not be able to benefit from initiatives that are based on an assumption that 16 and 17-year-olds live with their parents. Financial incentives may need to be tailored to their different circumstances.

- The different eligibility criteria and rules that govern programmes, services and benefits for this age group still create a maze that young people can find very hard to navigate. Variations in 'cut-offs and kick-ins' can make continuous participation hard to achieve.

question 5
What about the role and influence of family, peers, trusted adults and others close to young people?

We all have a range of significant people who exert an important influence on our life. This is as true for young people who are at risk of becoming NEET as it is for everyone else. For young people, these significant others include not just family members, but friends, peers and a potentially wide range of adults – teachers, mentors, personal advisers, learning personnel and employers, among others. Their influence can be positive or negative – and not uncommonly, a mixture of the two. For young people, families (and individual family members) can be supportive or alienating. There is strong evidence about the importance of parents' aspirations for their children, but some young people and their families may need help to work through strained relationships in order to maximise the potential support for the young person. Youth services are well placed to provide that help. Traditionally, this may not have been seen as part of their remit, but they do have a good record of working with parents – and they are not perceived as a threat, nor are they perceived as stigmatising in the way that statutory services often are.

parents and other relatives

Family poverty and unemployment have long been associated with poorer life chances for young people [53, 59]. Respondents to the consultation exercise commissioned for the Social Exclusion Unit's report *Bridging the Gap* highlighted the norm in many families of a long-standing lack of work opportunities and a belief that their prospects would not improve in the future [59]. The report concluded that the absence of a family history of work often deprives young people of optimism about the role of learning and denies them important practical knowledge, eg of how the job market operates, how to get a job and how to weigh up the pros and cons of different options. Parental poverty can also propel young people into low-paid work at the expense of their future prospects. And it can mean they leave home prematurely if work is not available. These home circumstances were reflected in the statistics about continuing education beyond school-leaving age – 91 per cent of young people from managerial or professional families stayed on at 16, compared with 61 per cent from unskilled families.

But it is important to recognise that the impact of parental attitudes and experiences are by no means wholly negative for less well-off families. For example, an analysis of data from a study of young people in receipt of Education Maintenance Allowance found that many parents had a positive attitude towards their children's continued education. Parents' support for their children's aspirations, even when young people had gained no qualifications, enabled young people to stay on at school. Ninety per cent of the parents of young people in the NEET group in the study recognised the value of qualifications in obtaining a decent job and leading to better long-term earnings. This was as true for parents with no qualifications as for the rest [57].

Research studies have explored other dimensions of the links between parental attitudes and circumstances, and opportunities and outcomes for their children. For example, the analysis of longitudinal data about cognitive and non-cognitive skills produced some conclusions that are relevant to any discussion of how best to intervene early to prevent young people becoming NEET. The study found an association between low socioeconomic status of fathers and truancy rates in children. It showed the importance for children's skill development of family background and the learning environment provided at home – by age seven, social class was exerting a significant impact on children's ability in both cognitive and social skills. And serious family difficulties (including divorce, and parental mental health and substance misuse problems) were associated with lower skills development at both age seven and eleven [9].

The study of young people's experience of organised after-school activities also highlights the role of parental interest or influence in children's decisions to engage in the first place – and then to stay involved [63].

These issues were explored in greater detail in the Fabian Society's broader study of non-formal activities. Its starting point was the key influence of background in determining one's chances of achieving good life outcomes [2]. By age six, children from disadvantaged backgrounds who demonstrated high ability as infants have been overtaken by children from more affluent backgrounds who demonstrated lower ability in infancy. The Fabian Society study identified various influences at play. Young people in a more advantaged position benefit from the educational resources and opportunities for development they have enjoyed, from the encouragement and support from parents and others, and from the absence of financial and cultural barriers to continued learning. The report argues that parental interest and involvement when children are young is an essential component of agency strategies to reduce the later low achievement of young people [50].

So it is not that children's life chances are immutable. Rather, it is important to focus on the obstacles facing people from disadvantaged communities in order to see what can be done to ensure that children have a more equal chance of reaching their full potential [56]. The impact on young people of intergenerational family and community unemployment is more likely to be addressed through initiatives that encourage input from parents [58].

peers

The Social Exclusion Unit identified two factors that are likely to deter young people from taking up training places and propel them instead towards taking 'dead-end' jobs: one is the prospect of being in debt (see Questions 2 and 4), the other is the pressure to conform with their peers [59].

The pressure exerted by friends can be negative or positive, however. The study of after-school activities concluded that having something to do offered young people new friendships and fresh and broader perspectives on behaviour, priorities and other issues. These friendships in organised clubs seemed to be a positive influence, as evidenced by discussion between participants about shared motivation and a shared commitment to improving skills [63]. But if the purpose is only to fill time, rather than about being active together, then the peer group may instead impose constraints on young people's learning and education – and those constraints may be considerable and far reaching.

One evaluation of non-formal learning argues that negative peer effects are the most significant risk associated with leisure activities – especially if the group meets in one place only and comprises young people at high risk of social exclusion and educational disengagement. The study suggests that strong peer relationships may constitute a form of 'bonding' social capital by bringing together people of similar attitudes and dispositions, but sometimes to the exclusion of other views and perspectives. The pull of these local relationships may prevent young people from moving away from an area to pursue education or career options, and may make group perspectives more entrenched [2].

In exploring ways of tackling the cultural forces which seem detrimental to young people's interests, the researchers point to the value in Northern Ireland of bringing different groups together, and of the benefit of having a trusted adult who could enable 'bridging' social capital to develop. This is about building bridges between groups with disparate or conflicting views.

So the challenge for youth work and other agencies is to help young people at risk of becoming NEET to broaden their horizons by putting new opportunities, experiences and contacts within their grasp. There is an advantage if young people can identify with youth workers from the same locality or background as themselves, because that can help overcome the negative influence of peers in the community.

Similar conclusions about the role and influence of peers are drawn by those evaluating the national programme of community projects that seek to deflect young people from NEET status [1]. A general conclusion is that peer influences can be a positive or negative force in young people's lives and that peer groups can have a significant impact on whether a young person moves from NEET to EET status.

Young people may find inspiration in joining a new activity or coming in contact with an adult who awakens interest or motivation. But it is difficult to alter someone's way in life if they remain in a neighbourhood or environment where negative influences prevail [64].

Connexions and personal advisers

The Connexions service has its origins in the Social Exclusion Unit's report on young people out of contact with learning or training – Bridging the Gap [59]. Connexions was established in April 2001, with a national unit and 47 local partnerships co-terminous with Learning and Skills Councils. The objective was to support young people aged 13 to 19 to make informed life choices. This help was to be offered through a one-stop personal guidance and integrated youth service based out of school, with a remit to support young people through the education and other life changes experienced in their teen years. An important element of this support was ensuring a smooth transition from compulsory schooling to post-16 learning.

It was hoped that Connexions would help remedy identified problems in the support mechanisms for young people – fragmented services with precarious funding arrangements, insufficient preparation in school for post-16 choices and a dearth of help for young people who were outside the relatively supportive world of school. An integral part of the concept was that personal advisers would offer young people an individualised service, forging close links with them and offering appropriate and timely support and challenge. In 2002, local partnerships were tasked to achieve (by 2004) a 10 per cent reduction in the proportion of young people NEET.

Does it work?

The National Audit Office report of 2004 found that Connexions was on track to meet its target to reduce the proportion of young people NEET. In addition, most young people surveyed said they had found the service helpful [49].

Aspects of the personal adviser system that worked particularly well were identified in another study. These included personal advisers being based at jobcentres and taking referrals from centre staff, intensive outreach delivered in a style that suited young people, a focus on soft skills (such as confidence, motivation, self-control and interpersonal skills) that helped boost engagement, and continued contact and support when placements collapsed [36].

mentoring

Mentoring was first promoted in the 1990s in two main ways – firstly, as a means of supporting student teachers on PGCE courses [3]; and secondly, by Education Business Partnerships to support young people during the last two years of compulsory schooling, particularly those considered 'borderline' for passing their GCSE examinations at grade C [30]. Mentoring then became a central element of the Youthstart Programme, which ran over four years in the mid-1990s as part of the European Commission's Employment Initiative. In this context, it was directed primarily at disaffected young people between the ages of 16 and 18 who were not in education, employment or training.

Since Labour came to power in 1997, various government departments have continued to promote mentoring as an integral element of diverse educational and social policies for social inclusion [13]. Young offenders and young people who are NEET, as well as young people thought to be at risk of entering either category, remain the main target groups. This has become known as 'engagement mentoring'.

Does it work?

On the whole, there is positive evidence of the benefits of mentoring, although the quantity and quality of research is weak. Among the small number of studies, some show statistically significant results but others show that mentoring has little or no measurable effect. The overall impression is that mentoring does benefit young people but the effect is small. At present, therefore, studies provide little evidence that mentoring can achieve outcomes such as re-integrating disadvantaged young people with mainstream education and work.

The evidence about small but significant effects [13, 15] relates to engaging young people who are NEET, reducing anger and violence, and improving confidence and self-esteem. But the effect of mentoring on reducing offending, increasing engagement in the community and improving academic performance is less well established. And while there is good evidence to support traditional mentoring, there is much less evidence to judge the effectiveness of peer mentoring or e-mentoring schemes.

Those behind mentoring schemes sometimes complain that they find it hard to demonstrate the effectiveness of their work, however. They argue that the benefits are often intangible and do not easily lend themselves to straightforward measurement. And whatever the weaknesses in the evidence base, anecdotal evidence indicates that mentoring can sometimes have a transforming effect on young people's lives.

Investment in training and support is key to good mentoring schemes. Regular contact between mentor and mentee over a sustained period of time is also important for a successful relationship. Good mentor selection, work with families and structured activities for young people and mentors are all important too. But mentoring can do harm as well as good – short relationships can be disruptive for the young person and can lead to a deterioration in behaviour. To date, there has been limited research into why mentoring relationships break down and the impact this has on the young people involved.

Despite its reliance on volunteers, mentoring is also relatively expensive, costing between £2,000 and £5,000 a year for each young person. Nevertheless, the government clearly thinks such investment is worthwhile, having allocated £7 million via HM Treasury, the Home Office and the Department for Education and Skills (now DCSF) between 2001 and 2006, with a further £1 million a year being provided to the Mentoring and Befriending Foundation as a long-term grant.

case examples

Peer tutors, Brighton and Hove

Some projects use peer tutors to mentor other young people. The Care2Share peer education programme in Brighton and Hove matches disengaged 16- to 25-year-olds with young adults in the same age range. They become their tutors, supporting the learners to achieve their goals using the internet and CDs and web-pages. Peer tutors also work alongside the young adults in developing practical skills, such as running a snack bar in the centre.

Buddy Reading Project, Derbyshire

Read On – Write Away! (ROWA!) works with local partners to develop a community literacy and basic skills strategy for Derbyshire and Derby City. It aims to improve levels of literacy and basic skills, especially among disadvantaged groups, and to improve workforce skills. Although it provides opportunities for people of all ages, a key strand of its work focuses on training young volunteers to support school-based learning. The Buddy Reading Project works with young adult volunteers aged 14 to 25 who are disengaged from learning. It trains them to support school pupils in their reading, while at the same time enhancing their own literacy skills and personal development. Another part of the project provides volunteer opportunities in a variety of educational settings, through activities such as buddy reading or writing, mentoring and lesson support.

others – employers and training providers

A report on regional differences in the number of those who are NEET in England offers some insights into the potential role of employers and training providers in improving outcomes for young people [58]. The study suggests that the potential of young people without traditional qualifications to enter the world of work seems restricted by the lack of awareness among employers of the range of qualifications awarded to young people and their equivalence to traditional qualifications such as GCSEs and A levels. Other employer-related factors for why young people become or stay disengaged were identified. These were about employers holding unrealistically high expectations of young people's abilities, a resistance to looking beyond personal or familiar sources for new employees, and lengthy application procedures that serve to demotivate young people rather than harness their interest quickly and with enthusiasm. The study concludes that employers need to become more engaged in finding ways of increasing opportunities for young people, by offering work-based learning opportunities and work placements.

The lack of such openings continues to pose real obstacles for young people's progress, and is a particular dilemma for older teenagers and for those living in rural areas. In the latter case, for example, there may be a college place for a young person wishing to pursue an Apprenticeship but no local employer willing to provide the vocational element needed. There is scope for closer liaison between training providers and local employers, and for making and taking opportunities to work together to pilot ideas from other places.

youth work

*This description of youth work comes from: *The National Youth Agency Research Programme Series: The contribution of youth work to the Every Child Matters Outcomes. Book 1 – Introduction. Leicester: The National Youth Agency*

Youth work helps young people by offering personal development, education and life skills programmes tailored to individual need, and by providing social, economic, educational and recreational opportunities designed to encourage social inclusion and life-long learning (NYA, 2006). Its contribution has a strong professional base. Merton and colleagues (2004) identified four main distinctive features of youth work. It is based on:

- voluntary engagement of young people
- young people's active involvement in different features of local youth provision
- use of informal education as a primary medium and method
- a flexible and responsive approach to provision.

According to Merton et al (2004), there is widespread consensus within the youth work profession that the core purpose of youth work is the personal and social development of young people through informal education. However, the study suggests that there is lack of clarity outside the youth work profession about what youth workers actually do. This is largely because many youth workers talk about their work in terms of its values rather than what it is meant to achieve.

Youth work is more strategic than is sometimes portrayed. Merton et al (2004) describe youth work activity as preventative, and point to its role in relation to social inclusion. The approach is a holistic one, in addressing the totality of a young person's experience in a social context. Depending on the individual circumstances of the young person (including their community and family contexts), youth work variously contributes to their re-integration, diversion and engagement in preventative activity, protection and enablement, levels of aspiration and achievement and active citizenship. Through youth work, young people are helped to prepare for working life.

Youth work helps young people maximise their potential. Davies (2005) stresses its commitment to 'a potentiality rather than a deficiency model' of young people. He argues that youth work provides a security and a facility which affirms 'more critical and creative responses' that can lead to change.

A fundamental element in the youth work value base is that young people set their own aims and objectives (Davies, 2005). This means that young people are listened to and their views respected. Engagement needs therefore to be on a voluntary basis. The flexibility and time perspectives of the service make it possible for young people to review and revise their earlier choices, allowing them to re-enter education and training, for example.

References

- Davies, B. (2005). 'Youth work: a manifesto for our times', Youth and Policy No 88.
- Merton, B. et al. (2004). An evaluation of the impact of youth work in England. DfES Research Report RR606.
- NYA (2006) The NYA Guide to Youth Work and Youth Services. Leicester, National Youth Agency.

*This can be found at: www.nya.org.uk/information/100584/researchpublications/ Accessed 29 August 2008.

Question 5 - Summary points

- A wide range of adults have the potential to influence young people's lives – not only parents and other family members, but also teachers, mentors, personal advisers, youth workers, activity leaders and employers, among others.

- Parents' aspirations for their children are important to young people's life chances – parents influence not only young people's attitudes towards education, but also their decisions on whether or not to engage with other positive social and learning activities. However, some families may need help to work through strained relationships in order to maximise the potential support available to young people.

- Peers are also a significant influence – both positive and negative. After and out-of-school activities can offer new friendships, new perspectives and new opportunities. Peer influence is more likely to be positive when organised groups meet to do something, rather than just kill time, and include young people with different experiences and outlooks.

- Investment in training and support is a key part of providing good mentoring schemes. Regular contact between mentor and mentee over a sustained period of time is also important – short relationships can be disruptive, although there has been limited research into why mentoring relationships break down and the impact this has on the young people involved.

- Employers can play a vital role in boosting the life chances of young people, yet that potential is often not utilised. Many have a poor understanding of the full range of qualifications awarded to young people and their significance – and many use drawn-out recruitment procedures that demotivate rather than engage young people. It is also important that more employers are persuaded to provide training opportunities and work placements.

question 6
What do we know about young people in different NEET groups?

The literature distinguishes, broadly, between young people who are NEET and those who are at risk of becoming NEET. Within these two umbrella groups young people are clustered into sub-groups, with variation in sub-group headings between different studies. Overall, they constitute what might be called 'a mixed bunch' in that some sub-groups describe the characteristics or circumstances of young people, others reflect the administrative categories used by agencies, still others cluster according to the young people's unmet needs. And there is, of course, overlap between the sub-groups, with many young people fitting under several headings.

The following list shows, in alphabetical order, the headings most commonly used in the reports scrutinised for this review:

- additional support needs – in response to developmental delay, disability, physical and mental health problems, limiting long-term illness
- adult and/or sibling care givers
- black and minority ethnic status
- care issues, including young people in care and those leaving care
- family disadvantage and poverty
- homeless young people
- refugee or asylum-seeker status
- substance misuse
- teenage mothers (or parents)
- young people in contact with the youth justice system.

What is striking in the literature is the similarity of risk factors that affect young people across the group as a whole. Young people in all the groups – no matter how commentators cluster them – are described as being 'vulnerable' or 'in need' or 'needing targeted or specialist support services' if they are to have as equal a chance as their peers of making good progress in life.

The recurring themes are summarised well in the report to government about young children with communication difficulties:

If a child does not benefit from early intervention there are multiple risks: of lower educational attainment, of behavioural problems, of emotional and psychological difficulties, of poor employment prospects and, in some cases, of a descent into criminality. [6]

From the other end of the age spectrum, what is deemed likely to have helped keep young people out of the youth justice system (by promoting their educational engagement and attainment) will be familiar to those with knowledge of promising early interventions for other young people and their families. These factors were identified in a study by the Youth Justice Board:

- pre-school education
- family literacy
- parenting information and support, and help to improve family relationships
- reasoning and social skills education
- organisational change in schools
- reading schemes
- maintaining attendance at school.

[66]

National data

CCIS[7] records a wide range of characteristics, including all those in the alphabetical list above (except 'family disadvantage and poverty' – although information for post code can be extracted). These data are analysed and used to plan and commission local services, but the Department for Children, Schools and Families does not publish this information because it is consent based. Four key groups are identified separately in the statistics used to monitor local authority performance, however. These are:

- teenage mothers
- learners with learning difficulties and/or disabilities (LDD)
- care leavers
- young people from black and minority ethnic groups (BME).

Promising approaches

What can be gleaned about promising approaches for young people in the different NEET sub-groups? It is worth repeating here the point made in the introduction, about the difficulty of mapping the effectiveness of specific interventions. As researchers have commented, this is a difficult area to unravel, because interventions have tended not to be introduced with specific NEET groups in mind, nor to address the particular problems that impede young people's progress in moving to EET status [64].

The point is also made that young people who are NEET are not a homogenous group. They come from a range of backgrounds. They have had a range of experiences. Some people's histories are complex, others less so. Resilience factors are as important as risk factors, and each of these factors has a different and changing impact on the life and the life chances of family members. And 'whilst there were risk

[7] The Client Caseload Information System (CCIS) is a database run by Connexions in local areas to record information about the young people they work with.

factors that seemed to predispose young people to becoming NEET, not all young people exposed to these risk factors had ended up in the NEET group' [57]. Similarly, some young people who become NEET do not come from any of the groups identified above.

With those caveats in mind, some lessons from the literature – about young people's circumstances and needs, and about policy and promising practice – are set out below. We focus mainly on the four groupings used by the Department for Children, Schools and Families, plus young people in the youth justice system as this group often features in local authority reports.

BME young people
Key messages about circumstances and needs

The literature points to the unequal access to participation by BME young people [58]. Those of African-Caribbean, Pakistani and Bangladeshi origin have longer periods out of learning than Indian and white young people. Those of Pakistani and Bangladeshi origin are particularly likely to experience lengthy spells of non-participation, with one in six of them having four or more months out of EET in their first two years after compulsory schooling. In 2005, Pakistani and Bangladeshi young people were more likely than white young people to be NEET at age 19 (with 16 per cent non-participating versus 10 per cent). But note that Indian young people are least likely to be so (only 5 per cent) by that age.

The school experience of BME young people is not equal either. African-Caribbean, Pakistani and Bangladeshi young people are less likely than other groups to get good examination results – in 2004, only 36 per cent of black-Caribbean and 43 per cent of black-African young adult learners gained five or more GCSE grades A-C or equivalent, compared to 52 per cent of white learners. And African-Caribbean young people were the ones most likely to be excluded from school.

Both these factors – lower attainment and lower attendance – are risk factors for young people becoming NEET after leaving school. Within overall improvements in attainment, particular concerns relate to Bangladeshi and Pakistani children (especially in the early years and in their lack of high grades), to African-Caribbean young people in secondary school, and to Gypsy and Traveller pupils and those from refugee communities [54].

There are implications here for education, employment and training providers. Approaches used in school were deemed to be part of the problem, with a marked lack of strategy for raising attainment or for monitoring comprehensively the progress made by BME pupils. Staff responses to this challenge were described as verging on helplessness. Despite this, BME pupils were more likely than white young people to be in full-time education beyond 16, and studying from a college rather than a school base.

Beyond formal education, BME young people face extra barriers to participation, and the impact of these is striking. They find it harder to access training – this is less likely to be obtained while in work or to lead to work, or to be their preferred choice. They are also more than twice as likely as white young people to be out of work during their older years beyond formal education. In 2000, unemployment rates were two to three times higher for young people aged 16 to 24 from minority ethnic backgrounds, irrespective of their educational attainment.

Key messages about practice and policy

The community-based programmes read for this review offer insights into the educational achievement and opportunities for BME young people. Interestingly, the evaluation of the largest of these programmes [1] found that BME young people were more likely than white young people to move to EET status – the success rate was 49 per cent for Asian and Chinese, 42 per cent for black, and 38 per cent for white young people. Conversely, two-thirds of Asian and Chinese young people, compared with just over half the group overall, had a low level of school achievement. White young people were almost twice as likely as BME young people to have long periods of non-participation. And white and black young people were more likely than their Asian or Chinese peers to be in or on the edge of the youth justice system. The evaluators offer no explanation or observation on these findings, some of which buck the trend according to the national statistics presented above.

The evaluation also looked at the shift in attitudes of participants. They found that programmes delivered to mixed groups of white and BME young people produced no shift in attitude from the prevailing 'us and them' feeling. The evaluators concluded that long-term work, perhaps supported by specific funding streams, might help address such ethnic division.

case example

The Aspire Project, Brent

The Aspire Project provided a service to black young men of African-Caribbean descent who had been referred to Brent's Tier-3 specialist Child and Adolescent Mental Health Service (CAMHS). The service was intended to help CAMHS provide the young men with culturally sensitive support to enhance their emotional health and well-being and prevent further escalation into higher-level mental health services.

The project recruited and trained volunteer mentors, supported the mentors in this specialist work and acted as a link between the young men and CAMHS. The mentors' role was to help the young people in their life choices, to support their family and carers, and to help develop a local support system for the young people. An element of the holistic response to need was ensuring that each young person developed a career profile, with plans for further study and/or work.

Aspire was able to respond quickly to young people's acute distress, providing intensive support for as long as it was needed. That intensity was reduced over time as the young person settled down. A feature of the project was the ability of staff to 'hang on in there and go at the young person's pace'. They helped young people remain at home rather than be admitted to psychiatric care, and they helped fathers in particular renew contact with their child and take on an active role in their life.

There were gains in terms of young people's EET status too. Project staff organised opportunities for young people to talk to local employers about how to pursue their particular career interests, encouraged them to establish a daily routine for themselves, and – despite the severity and complexity of the young people's difficulties – helped some of them return to part or full-time education.

young people leaving care

Key messages about circumstances and needs

A disproportionate number of young people who have recently left care, or who are still in care, are not in education, training or work that offers good training prospects.

Three-quarters of care leavers (as opposed to six per cent of the general population of the same age) have no academic qualifications. Many fewer than their peers, only 12 to 19 per cent, move on to full-time education, and only half the young people in leaving-care projects are in work.

Young people leaving care face similar obstacles to participation as others who are NEET – 19 per cent are from BME groups (compared to six per cent of the general population), a fifth are likely to be homeless within two years of leaving care and care leavers are more likely to be depressed, self-harm or have an eating disorder. In addition, they face particular difficulties such as a lack of family support, an expectation (from the local authority, their corporate parent) that they will live independently from an earlier age than young people raised at home, and an unsettled educational and home background.

Comparing care leavers with other young people of their age, the Care Matters Implementation Plan highlighted the injustice.

> They are five times less likely to achieve five good GCSEs and eight times more likely to be excluded from school. They are less likely to go to university and more likely to end up in prison. [24]

One proposal of direct relevance to young people who are NEET (and included in the Children and Young Persons Bill currently before parliament) is increased direct support for young people in or returning to education, with access to a personal adviser up to the age of 25. The aim is to help young people overcome the barriers they face and make a lasting difference to their lives.

Key messages about practice and policy

In relation to continued formal learning, the government is pursuing various proposals to boost the support and encouragement that might help more care leavers make the move into further and higher education. These include: extra support at the admissions stage and the start of courses; making available grants and bursaries, and loans with deferred repayment arrangements; and offering vacation accommodation at their place of study or in their home area. At university level, there will be mentoring from older students and efforts to increase staff awareness and support for young people's particular needs.

Some of the other practice messages about young people leaving care are relevant for work around learning and employment. In particular, it is important to ensure that young people feel well supported, both emotionally and practically, so they can benefit from and enjoy the challenges ahead of them. A number of factors can help create a stable base from which young people are able to move on – having safe and decent housing, help with finances, continued links with carers and families, access to local health services, and someone to turn to at times of stress [24].

As for other NEET groups, there are messages about preventing young people becoming NEET. Young people still in care need sound information and advice in school about their options. It is important that foster carers and residential staff provide young people in care with an education-rich environment. Careful overview by a senior officer, of both individual needs and available options, is essential, as is an ongoing analysis of young people's journeys after compulsory schooling in order to help inform the development of the support and resources provided.

A local authority's support can also extend beyond that of corporate parent. As well as having joint or sole parental responsibility for the children in their care, local authorities are in an excellent position as large employers to offer these young people work-related placements.

case examples

A young person's experience

Kate was referred to the personal adviser when she was eight months pregnant, after concealing the pregnancy for a long time. She had learning difficulties and had been involved with social services because of past abuse. The personal adviser helped support Kate before her baby was born and liaised with the social worker to ensure Kate knew what was being planned. The personal adviser went to a child protection meeting with Kate and helped her feel more able to talk in a room full of strangers. Kate's baby was born prematurely and Kate was taken to a mother and baby unit in another area. Her personal adviser stayed in touch with both Kate and the social worker. The baby was later placed in foster care, with Kate allowed limited contact. The personal adviser supported Kate throughout this time, including helping Kate access sexual health advice and raising the possibility of her returning to college. She also arranged a voluntary placement in a children's charity shop. In due course, Kate returned to college while still working in the charity shop.

Acting as a good parent

Lewisham council offers young people moving on from care the chance of a traineeship within services run by the council, giving them the chance to build up skills and experience to help secure later employment. The young people spend a year working in Environmental Services on a range of areas including plumbing, carpentry, electrical work and administration. During their year they gain a strong foundation in key skills and learn how to apply for jobs and operate effectively in a work environment. They also attend Lewisham College on day release.

teenage parents

Key messages about circumstances and needs

Overall, there is a strong link between NEET status and becoming a young (often single) parent. Early parenthood is associated with poverty, a lack of access to good-quality work and, in time, poorer outcomes for the children involved.

Most of what is written and said about being a young parent relates to young mothers rather than fathers. About one in five (a total of 30,000) young women who are NEET have caring responsibilities for their child, and a third of teenage mothers are not in learning or work before becoming a parent. Furthermore, two-thirds of young women who are NEET for at least six months between the ages of 16 and 18 have a baby by age 21, compared with less than a fifth of other young women.

Young parents may find it particularly difficult to continue their education, because they may be excluded during their pregnancy or they may drop out because the birth has interrupted their schooling. Later, the lack of child care or the stress of coping with a baby may make it hard to re-engage with learning or pursue work options. On the other hand, having a baby can be a motivating factor for young parents and can bring new peers and adults into their life. The literature cautions against accepting the media messages that portray teenage parenthood in negative light, and as a social norm for specific groups [26].

Key messages about practice and policy

Pregnancy brings numerous new things to think about, including care during the pregnancy, how to parent, and sorting out benefits and housing. For young parents, there is the question of balancing the needs and responsibilities of having a new baby with how to meet their own needs and aspirations as a teenager. And then there is the question of whether (and how) to return to education or move on to work or other learning. On this last point, the literature has more to say about promising approaches to service responses to these needs than about validated intervention programmes.

- **Specialist advisers** These play a crucial role in providing co-ordinated and trusted support to young parents. There are concerns, however, about changes to the Connexions service and its transfer to local authority management – in particular, that some dedicated services for young people who are NEET, such as specialist advisers to young parents, may be cut.

- **Housing and benefits** The lack of permanent affordable accommodation is a particular problem for young mothers moving on from temporary housing. Some local authorities are moving young mothers to expensive private sector rented accommodation for which the high rent is covered by housing benefit, as long as the mother is not in work. But if the mother were to get a job, housing benefit would be discontinued and the wages may not cover the rent. This discourages young people from going to work, thus locking them in the poverty trap as they cannot risk losing their housing. We also need to know more about the type of housing young parents are living in, including how many are homeless.

- **Child care** The Care to Learn scheme helps fund child care so that parents are able to return to education, employment or training. The scheme has been evaluated recently (as explained in Question 4).

- **Projects for young parents** These work well because they take a holistic approach to working with young mothers. What seems particularly beneficial is employing tutors who have empathy with the young people and excellent interpersonal and communication skills. This may be more important than having a subject specialist. Tutors need to offer encouragement to the young people to progress into work through a range of different possible routes.

- **Information about fathers** Although data collected through CCIS includes information on young mothers and their engagement in education or training, we know very little about young men aged 16 plus, especially those who are NEET, including those who are young fathers. The literature has very little to tell us in this respect. (This information is sought through CCIS. However, since CCIS is a consent-based system it is dependent on a young man disclosing that he is a father and then agreeing to that information being recorded.)

case examples

Young mothers' project, West Bassetlaw

At the Sure Start project in West Bassetlaw, the main motivation for young mothers to attend learning activities is to mix with other young parents and share experiences. An outreach centre is based in the middle of a nearby housing estate and young mothers can drop in and talk to each other and the social worker on site. This is a spur to their engagement with the project and the learning opportunities it offers. These focus on family learning, health and life skills. They include facilities that respond to the young mothers' needs – parent and toddler groups, a toy library and baby clinics – as well as customised programmes directly relevant to their concerns: Bumps, Babies and Babble, Wednesday Women and Toddler Time. The centre offers learning activities for parents and children together (mainly through play) and separately. More recently, family learning activities have been developed with Early Start sessions for 0 to 3s, which encourage language and communication development. A weekly computer session, led by the Sure Start learning co-ordinator and using LearnDirect resources, is held in the local village hall, to help parents improve their literacy, language and numeracy skills.

Developing Dads in Rotherham

This scheme started by employing a father-worker manager at the YMCA, two outreach workers and a volunteer hoping to become a youth worker. The team of workers has developed new skills. As well as accompanying young fathers at court and jobcentre meetings, they have encouraged them to contribute to presentations at conferences and take part in group work activity sessions around being a father. The team has also become expert in parental rights and responsibilities and has networked with other professionals to promote the work of the project. Much of this has been learned by doing and has enhanced the personal and social development of the young fathers who use the project.

young people with learning difficulties and/or disabilities (LDD[8])

Key messages about circumstances and needs

Young people with learning difficulties are more than six times as likely as their peers to be excluded from school, and they are much more likely to leave school without qualifications. Inevitably, then, they are over-represented in the population of young people who are not participating in work or learning. They are twice as likely to be unemployed as other young people. In some areas, those who have the greatest need of intensive support in school for their special educational needs (ie, being at School Action Plus) have an unemployment rate that is four times higher than other pupils [33].

Those with physical disabilities face similar disadvantage – young people with a serious health problem or disability are more likely than their peers not to continue in education or move to work on leaving school at 16. By 18, a quarter of these young people are not participating in such activity. And they are three times as likely as other young people to be NEET at 19.

The overall situation is that young people with disabilities or learning difficulties are twice as likely as other young people to be NEET [21].

The striking need is for these young people to have fair access to the opportunities enjoyed by their peers. They need the chance to choose from a wide range of educational opportunities and to gain entry to courses that will enable them to follow their dreams. They need teachers who will have high expectations of what they can achieve, and employers who understand their circumstances and do not discriminate against them. They need existing physical and attitudinal barriers to be broken down, and choice and control over the assistance they receive. Both they and their families need information and support to help them meet new people, make friends, have fun and make a smooth transition to adulthood [35].

Key messages about practice and policy

There are some common messages about promising or effective services in response to the needs of this group of vulnerable young people. These have been incorporated into the Youth Taskforce Action Plan, which builds on the government's commitment outlined in the Children's Plan.

- Preparation for leaving school should start early, at Key Stage 3.

- School records, including assessments of need, should follow the young person as they move on, with post-16 support continuing to age 19 at least.

---

[8] Under the Learning and Skills Act 2000 a person has a learning difficulty if they have a significantly greater difficulty in learning than the majority of persons of their age, or they have a disability which either prevents or hinders them from making use of facilities of a kind generally provided by institutions providing post-16 education or training.

- Financial incentives, such as EMAs, should be adapted in order to cater for young people's specific learning and employment needs.
- There should be increased recognition by personal advisers of learning difficulties and of how to access both assessment and support services.
- Training providers should be funded to recognise the needs of young people formally indentified as having special educational needs. [22]

case example

Choices Project, Cheshire

Choices aims to ensure equality of opportunity for young people with learning difficulties, to fulfil their potential as individuals as well as members of groups and communities, and to support them during the transition to adulthood. The youth work focuses on young people's views about what is relevant to them in their development, and informal educational programmes are developed with this in mind. The project meets weekly and is open to 13- to 25-year-olds. Provision for those aged 13 to 15 focuses on group activities where young people can develop their social skills, make new friends and gain social confidence. Provision for 16- to 18-year-olds continues to offer group activities but stresses individual development and the fostering of independent living skills. Young people are given opportunities to gain more confidence by taking on responsibility and making decisions. Provision for over-18s focuses on individual support and development with a view to young people moving on from Choices to make the most of other local opportunities. Activities are about having fun and raising expectations.

young people supervised by the youth offending service

Key messages about circumstances and needs

The literature highlights the challenges that face this group. They are a group most likely to be NEET over extended and repeated periods – at any one time, as few as one third of young people in the youth justice system are in full-time EET [66]. They can be harder than other groups to motivate. They find it harder than others to be accepted by mainstream services and their offending behaviour serves as a barrier to their finding and keeping work.

There is a strong association between offending behaviour and NEET status – 75 per cent of 16- to 17-year-old males before the youth court are in no formal full-time activity at that time. Four-fifths have been unemployed for more than six months, and the rest have never worked. Their offending behaviour is likely to have started earlier (sometimes much earlier), but having no regular activity in their mid to late teens substantially increases the opportunity for their being involved in crime.

There are serious concerns about the low level of education and attainment of young people sentenced to custody – two-thirds are at NVQ Level 1 or below for reading, and over three-quarters for writing and numeracy. This makes it all the more important to address the unsatisfactory nature of education and training in secure settings (especially for those held in Young Offender Institutions).

Key messages about practice and policy

High priority must be given to the EET needs of young people in the youth justice system. Specifically, young people need a core curriculum that is applied properly, someone to take a keen interest in exploring with them career and work options, suitable education and training placements available near the end of custody, and support in preparing for release into the community. It is also important to learn from the research evidence, including the finding that intensive provision of at least 36 hours per week can make a positive impact on young people's grasp of basic skills [7].

An important initiative for this review is a project run jointly by the Youth Justice Board and Connexions [67], which was designed to help achieve their shared target of 90 per cent of young offenders being in EET during and at the end of their sentence. Between 2003 and 2006, £8m was provided in 13 areas to fund personal advisers, mentors and strategic staff. The aim of the project was to understand the issues around movement from NEET to EET for this group of young people, and to learn the practice and policy implications.

The young people valued the personal support they received – they liked the relaxed and open approach of practitioners and mentors, and they liked having someone to talk to and trust. Those doing the work were valued by colleagues for being able to respond quickly and flexibly to young people, and for the sharing of information and knowledge that they helped promote with local employers and training providers.

But overall, the impact on levels of engagement was small. The reasons were to do with both the circumstances of the young people and the structural aspects of what was expected and provided.

Inevitably, the young people themselves were troubled and challenging. A quarter had special educational needs and a third had negative attitudes to engagement or had been permanently excluded from school. Their previous experiences, plus their offending behaviour and custodial sentences, had a negative impact on the development of educational skills and experiences. The young people thought that being EET would make a difference to their life, not least because it would occupy their time and give them money from a legitimate source. But they had to contend with recurring problems of peer influences, their substance misuse, further offending, family and accommodation difficulties and ingrained attitudes about education.

For staff and agencies, there was an ongoing tension between the target of speedy engagement or re-engagement in EET and the lack of structure in a young person's life. A realistic target was not full-time engagement but small steps (some forward, some backwards) on the long process of preparation for work. In other words, this is not about quick or cheap fixes but about providing long-term and child-centred support for young people beyond their custodial and community sentence, via staff who are working from a well-funded stable base.

A sobering conclusion of the study was that 'interruptions to programmed education, training and employment and frequent non-completion of courses disrupted and often ultimately sidelined the learning process'.

case examples

Promoting engagement through a youth inclusion project

Staff at a youth inclusion project negotiated an arrangement with young people and their parents whereby the project would provide opportunities for engagement in activities, such as learning how to mix music or coach football, in return for the monitoring of the young people's behaviour and their attendance at school. Results of the project show that engagement led to improved pupil performance and reduced offending behaviour.

A young person's experience

Helen was homeless and had been sleeping rough. Her boyfriend was several years older and was in prison. Helen had committed offences and was under the supervision of the Youth Offending Team (YOT). Because of the chaos in her life, she failed to attend appointments with both the YOT and Connexions. Helen was awaiting a room in a hostel via a local voluntary agency and admitted to having drug misuse issues and being concerned about her mental health. She had neither ID nor a bank account and it was feared she might be involved in prostitution. Her personal adviser attended an interview for benefits with Helen, who subsequently received Jobseeker's Allowance, and also helped her set up a temporary post office account to receive the benefit. The personal adviser referred Helen to a GP who arranged help from the community psychiatric nurse. Helen secured the promised room in the hostel but was later evicted because she was unable to stick to the house rules. The personal adviser made strenuous efforts to keep in touch with Helen, who by now was in breach of her supervision order and at risk of receiving a custodial sentence.

Question 6 - Summary points

- Young people who are NEET are not a homogenous group. Although a number of identifiable risk factors make it more likely that young people will become NEET, not all young people exposed to those risk factors do so. They come from a range of backgrounds and have had a range of experiences.

- Beyond formal education, young people from black and minority ethnic groups face extra barriers to participation. They find it harder to access training – this is less likely to be obtained while they are in work, to lead to work or to be their preferred choice. Robust advocacy on their behalf may help break down these additional barriers.

- Young people leaving care are likely to need considerable practical and emotional support in making the transition to further or higher education, training or employment. As well as supporting transitions in their role as corporate parent, local authorities are ideally placed to support care leavers through the offer of work placements and employment opportunities.

- Child care is critical to enabling young parents to continue with or re-engage in learning. Young mothers respond well to a holistic approach that addresses the broader context of their lives and helps them with practical problems. For many, being able to mix with other young parents in an informal setting, such as a drop-in centre, can be a spur to taking up new learning opportunities. Service providers may need to pay particular attention to the needs of young fathers, however – they are easily overlooked.

- Support to help young people with learning difficulties and/or disabilities make a successful transition from school into EET should begin early, during Key Stage 3. Assessments of need should follow young people as they move on and continue to age 19 at least. Providing young people with tailored financial incentives and funding training providers to cater for the special needs of this group can be particularly beneficial.

- Young people supervised by the youth offending service have particular needs – including tailored individual support that adequately addresses their career and work options, and provides suitable education and training places at the end of custody. However, the difficulties they face are often multiple and entrenched – agencies may need to identify a succession of practical, small steps to help them move forward.

question 7
What works during transition?

Youth is a phase, not always precisely defined, in the life-course between childhood and adulthood. Coles [11] sees youth transitions as having three main dimensions: the move from full-time education into the labour market (the school-to-work career); the attainment of (relative) independence from family of origin (the family career); and the move away from the parental home (the housing career). In recent decades, the effects of globalisation and de-industrialisation have resulted in these youth transitions becoming extended. The traditional concept of a rapid transition from school to work for working-class young people was already being questioned in the early 1970s. For example, Bazalgette [4] found that young people in Coventry were finding it increasingly difficult to make the transition because local networks that had traditionally been used to gain employment and housing were breaking down. He proposed the development of a new adult role, which he called the 'working coach' (what would now presumably be called a mentor), as a means of supporting transition.

By the mid-1970s, an earlier 'birth bulge' meant that larger than usual cohorts of young people were appearing on the labour market. This led to the development of various government schemes (for example the Youth Opportunities Programme and the Youth Training Scheme) intended to ease the inevitably extended transition for those young people without formal qualifications or who were living in parts of the country that were particularly affected by structural change, such as the loss of manufacturing industry. These schemes continued throughout the 1980s.

In the late 1990s the explicit connection was made once again between youth unemployment and the need for guidance, as well as training. As we have seen, a major concern of the Social Exclusion Unit's reports in 1999 [59] and 2005 [53] was the inequality of young people's experiences as they moved on from school.

While most young people enjoy a fairly smooth transition from school to work, often passing through A levels and university, a large minority lack support or guidance and clear pathways to take them along the way to good jobs and career opportunities [59].

Those who did best at school were able to develop clear goals and make smooth progress to further study elsewhere, before securing work and the prospect of career development. Or they remained at school and moved on to a job or structured training.

Those who fared worst at school, however, lacked the qualifications to enter these routes – or else personal and family problems got in the way, so that their journey lacked clarity in terms of goals and at points of key transition. In 1999, young school leavers ended up with less structure than was offered to unemployed older young people by the

New Deal. They were unlikely to find employment with good pay and prospects, and were at high risk of dropping out of work and failing to acquire the skills needed to hold their own in the workplace. Lacking further education or training opportunities, their future would consist of short-term jobs of poor quality, a lack of purposeful activity and social exclusion [59].

A later study [41] explored the range of 'mainstream' and 'alternative' careers that young people evolved in one small area experiencing severe socioeconomic deprivation in North-East England. This study examined six important 'careers' that make up youth transitions:

- school-to-work career
- family career
- housing career
- leisure career
- drug-using career
- criminal career.

The study found young people's transitions to be complex, non-linear, often disorderly and sometimes unpredictable. Many were still experiencing complicated transitions in which they struggled to reach the normal goals associated with adulthood – for instance, many had been unable to find lasting and rewarding employment.

Summarising much recent youth research, Jones [42] stresses the hardening up of this 'youth divide' and the social polarisation of young people's experiences and life chances. Those who make the speediest transitions into a youth labour market that has virtually 'collapsed', to parenthood and to independent living, face far greater risks of the negative outcomes associated with social exclusion.

The study characterises this polarisation as being about slow and fast-track transitions. Young people following the slow track stay in education and training, deferring entry to full-time work and deferring also the transition to new domestic and family formations. Many of these young people are from middle-class backgrounds where there is an expectation of continued support. Many young people from working-class backgrounds are having to adapt to these middle-class patterns, but with varying success.

Young people following a fast-track transition, on the other hand, commonly leave education without qualifications, try and enter a diminished youth labour market and start family formation transitions earlier. In many respects, these young people are trying to follow longstanding working-class practices – in other words, they are doing what their parents did. The problem is that youth incomes no longer support this type of transition. This group are more at risk of various forms of social exclusion, including homelessness, unemployment and teenage parenthood. They are also likely to experience 'protection deficit' – ie they are unable to receive adequate support from any source.

Those most at risk of social exclusion tend to come from the minority fast-track group, but include also young people who fail to negotiate the slower track successfully – often because of lack of financial support. This has implications for the identification of vulnerable groups, which are not always the most visible or easy to target for services.

What works?

In its final report Transitions: Young adults with complex needs (2005), the Social Exclusion Unit set out five key principles for service delivery for young adults that they believed were indicated by the evidence gathered [53]. Services should:

- actively manage the transition from youth to adult services
- take thinking and behaviour into account, and build on it
- involve young adults (and their families and carers) in designing and delivering services
- give effective information about services, and share information between services
- offer young people a trusted adult who can both challenge and support them.

The literature indicates a range of other factors that will help young people negotiate transitions successfully. These are described below.

Sustained support over time Young people need consistent access to help and support over time, rather than episodes of one-off advice. Support is particularly needed during the transitions from school at 16 and from youth to adulthood at 18 plus [50].

Help across service boundaries It is important to maintain an overview of a young person's needs in their entirety and to provide the appropriate support. This means identifying and meeting not just education and training needs, but also other needs that will impede education and training if they are not dealt with. Young people commonly need help to break down external barriers to learning (eg, cultural and financial) and internal barriers (eg, dispositions and horizons), which may prevent them from recognising and taking up opportunities.

Help for change in the modern world The transitions that young people have to negotiate today are very different to those that their parents' and grandparents' generations had to manage. They are more complex and call for a range of soft skills, such as confidence, motivation, self-control and interpersonal skills. Development of these skills will help prepare young people to cater for the twists and turns of life.

Help with stability as circumstances change Young people respond well to people who know them and to people who are valued by those close to them. The support provided by local people and small organisations is often underestimated – they can act as advocates on behalf of young people and be prepared to stick with a young person because they have known them a long time. This may be the only experience of stability a young person has experienced. It is through daily involvement in the neighbourhood that important contacts and networks are built and the circumstances of young people and their families understood. This is about building social capital – developing the networks of friendship, neighbourhood and trust that bind communities together [65].

Help through age-related transitions Although age is a poor indicator of individual economic need, a young person's age can have an impact on many areas of financial entitlement – for example, to benefits and the minimum wage. Age barriers can also affect access to services and at times when young people are most at risk. The Social Exclusion Unit (2005) sought to resolve some of these issues by defining a set of principles (see above) that should underpin services for young adults [53]. Some age-related transitions are particularly critical for young people with intensive support needs – for example, the transition from primary to secondary school. Continued support here can prevent a crucial drop in confidence and motivation, and consequent disengagement and disaffection, during Key Stage 3 (from 11 to 14 years) [58].

Information, advice and guidance (IAG) One of the key themes to emerge when looking at the NEET subgroups (see Questions 5 and 6) was the significance of weak family and support 'networks' and the role that important 'others' play in young people's lives. Information, advice and guidance – both when offered formally by service providers, and informally by peers and family – appears to have a significant influence on young people's decision making during transitions. This point was reinforced by the Social Exclusion Unit's 2005 report [53]. The new responsibility on local authorities to provide key Connexions services offers an opportunity to ensure that services are tailored to local needs, and that personal advisers are well supported in their IAG role [55].

Seizing opportunities One crucial thing to remember is that every transition provides an opportunity for those supporting young people to think afresh and to reappraise the situation. In a study of outcomes from a community-based employment programme, for example, Evans shows that for people who have been marginalised, a change in circumstances, such as gaining accommodation, can prompt a desire to learn and move on [28].

case examples

Paving the way to learning

To help young adults engage positively in learning sessions, the Nacro service in Newcastle undertakes priority work about their immediate support needs. The service has an on-site welfare officer who works with the young adults to help stabilise their situation, dealing with lack of housing, financial crisis or relationship breakdown. It is not expected that young adults will be able to engage positively in learning until these issues are addressed.

Legal advice to support transition

Streetwise Community Law Centre is a specialist legal advice service for 13- to 25-year-olds in South-East London. It employs young people's lawyers alongside youth workers, Connexions personal advisers and counsellors, and offers free advice, advocacy and representation on areas such as housing, benefits, education, employment rights and debt. An impact report found that getting access to expert legal advice makes a big difference to young people's life chances. Success factors for the centre included its location in a youth project, strong partnerships with youth workers, and the establishment of a formal network including youth service managers.

Question 7 - Summary points

- Transitions to adulthood are markedly different and more complex for young people than they were for their parents' and grandparents' generations. Many traditional routes to work and independent living have evolved or broken down. There is a greater need for young people to develop 'soft skills' – such as confidence, motivation, self-control and interpersonal skills – and to be able to cope with unforeseen twists and turns rather than a linear pathway.

- Sustained help and guidance over time, rather than one-off advice sessions, are more likely to help young people negotiate transitions successfully – especially when provided from within a holistic approach that identifies barriers to learning, as well as training and learning needs.

- Information, advice and guidance – both offered formally by service providers and informally by friends and family – appear to have a significant influence on the decisions young people make during transition. Providing informed advice and guidance, for example through Connexions, can be critical to young people reaching the right decisions.

question 8

Are there lessons to be learnt from projects aimed at helping adults back into work?

The programmes we have found in the literature are discussed below – they focus on work incentives from government, and comprehensive support from the voluntary sector to help people re-engage with the labour market.

incentives from government – New Deal for Young People

The New Deal for Young People is a national programme for young adults aged 18 to 24 that was introduced in January 1998 as part of the government's welfare to work strategy. The aim of the programme is to make young adults 'employable and employment ready' by helping those who have been in receipt of Jobseeker's Allowance for over six months to find work, acquire new skills or gain work experience. There is no extra payment for joining the scheme – on the contrary, benefit ceases if a place is not accepted, so in that sense it is not strictly an incentive. However, some would argue that the support offered can act as an incentive for young adults who are struggling to move on in their life. Structured support is delivered in three stages:

1 Gateway – this first stage lasts four months, during which time a young adult receives support from a personal adviser in applying for jobs.

2 Options – this stage lasts for at least 13 weeks and entails entry to further education or training, taking up a subsidised job, working on a community environment project, or working for a voluntary organisation.

3 Follow through – for those who have still not found a job, this final stage can last up to 26 weeks; extra help and further support with job searches are offered.

Does it work?

In 2004 the Social Exclusion Unit reported that the New Deal had contributed significantly both to a fall in unemployment (of 40,000) and to the increased possibility of a participant moving out of unemployment [52]. Where those at the lower end of the age group remained unemployed for up to a year after participation, they were more likely to move into training or education rather than work.

Commentators have argued for the need for more and better data to understand the outcomes for those participating in the programme, however. They also point to concerns that the state of the labour market means that making young adults employable will not be sufficient to guarantee them a place at the end of a programme [64].

There is also evidence that a drop in the unemployment rate after the introduction of the scheme was caused, in part, by young adults ceasing to claim benefit because they were deterred by the prospects of the compulsory nature of the scheme, which they did not envisage would be helpful in their search for work. And there is also evidence that some young adults were more likely to move into work only after their second or third spell of the programme [42].

incentives from government – Pathways to Work

This was a pilot programme that aimed to increase the number of recipients of incapacity benefit moving towards or into paid work. A weekly payment of £20 (the Job Preparation Premium – JPP) was paid for a maximum of 26 weeks to claimants doing some form of activity related to paid work.

Did it work?

The evaluation of the programme concluded that the supplement to benefit did not act as an incentive for people who were not already motivated to undertake a work-related activity – but it did sometimes act as further encouragement for people who were undecided about doing activities, or who were worried about the financial consequences of doing so [51]. Pathways to Work had a positive impact on some people, boosting their motivation and confidence, as well as helping them stay involved in activities. Most people felt they had made progress towards employment, and most found a way of continuing with activities after the payment ended .

employment and training support from the voluntary sector – Bootstrap Enterprises

Around the time that the Social Exclusion Unit report [59] about young people who were NEET was published in 1999, a survey was being planned to evaluate a voluntary sector employment and training project that had run for eight years, offering support to unemployed adults in a local area [28]. This was Bootstrap Enterprises, based in East London. The report of the survey provides some information about young people's experiences, as well as drawing conclusions about effective practice with older people who lived in a deprived neighbourhood and wanted to improve their job prospects.

The target group were the long-term unemployed or low-wage earners, disaffected young people, lone parents, and those facing discrimination or having special needs or few qualifications. Two-thirds of the 134 people in the sample group had qualifications at or below Level 1. Most were from a black or minority ethnic group.

The group had many features in common with young people who are NEET. Almost all had experienced problems at school – they spoke of mixing with the wrong crowd, messing about in lessons, bunking off, getting into trouble, being bullied, feeling uninspired and being treated unfairly. They were distracted, too, by life events in their early teenage years, especially family difficulties brought about by parental divorce, death or serious illness. None recalled being offered help with these problems from any source.

Did it work?

Despite the many barriers facing this particular group of job seekers, the outcomes were positive. Nearly two-thirds moved into a job. Their progress was also largely sustained over subsequent years, with some progressing over time to higher-paid work, a better-quality job and improved qualifications. Participants reported that they had gained in confidence, determination and ambition and felt a high level of satisfaction with the organisation.

Evaluation of the project suggests a number of lessons that might be relevant for younger people who are NEET. All these messages were as relevant to the small number of young people using the Bootstrap service as to the young adults and older clients in the service.

- **The ethos and approach of staff** – The evaluation concluded that the way people were treated was as important in creating and sustaining change as the service itself. Clients valued the encouragement and respect they were shown, the caring approach of staff and their general support, and the long-term follow up that was offered. Clients felt that staff really wanted them to succeed and would do all they could to make that happen.

  Staff views mirrored these comments. The ethos of the organisation was a strong belief in its own ability to help people take control of their life, and a willingness to innovate, take risks and learn from both success and failure. Staff had a clear understanding of the way in which family circumstances and experiences of school can have an enduring impact on job prospects, and be as relevant as childcare, health and transport problems. They set out to handle problems in a supportive, non-punitive way and they placed high value on fostering an atmosphere of mutual support, personal responsibility and respect for oneself and others. Their approach was driven, in part, by knowing how the disrespect shown by other agencies had hampered people's progress and knowing how important it is to find ways of helping people overcome their mistrust of statutory services.

- **The model of intervention** – The service offered holistic support to help people feel ready to move on in their work life. Confidence to get going, or to try again, was seen as crucial – so provision was varied and flexible, starting with practical activity that was low risk (in the sense that it did not need a big commitment and had a low chance of personal failure). Entry to employment services were open to anyone who wanted to improve their job prospects, followed by customised training, work experience and job links for those who felt more job ready. There was a focus on 'soft skills'

The outreach approach meant that contact could be made with the most needy and isolated people and assurance given that they would be welcome to join in with activities. The neighbourhood base for employment and training advice and resources also helped draw people in, as did the offer of child care and travel expenses when needed.

The service aimed to be client centred and did so by ensuring that one person acted as a client's key contact (the equivalent of a key worker, or lead professional under the ECM agenda). There was close support and detailed monitoring, to keep tabs on an individual's progress and determine next steps, including referral to specialist agencies.

• **The wider context** – A strong message from this study is that the emphasis on job outcomes – by both welfare-to-work and local funding schemes – can make it hard to meet the needs of this group of unemployed people. Training that leads to real jobs encourages the cynical, and work experience (ideally paid) encourages those with plenty of training but little experience of work. Much is to be gained by getting local people into local jobs, and an organisation that develops good links with employers in the area is well placed to help people take difficult first steps on the road to work – as well as ensuring that other job seekers can benefit from a wide range of possible options.

Another message to emerge is that once someone is in a low-paid job, it becomes increasingly difficult to access affordable careers advice, support, training or further education that could lead to further progress. This points to the need for in-work financial support to underpin a policy that supports the take up of low-income, high-insecurity jobs.

• **Building on motivation** – A final message is that those who were most successful had reached a point in their life where they needed things to change. A voluntary, rather than a compulsory, service response was most helpful for them. So, too, was the support that continued after a job was secured. Clients were particularly appreciative of the quarterly follow up from Bootstrap and the repeated message that they could return at any time.

If those things are in place there is a greater chance of helping people overcome some of the key barriers to employment – poor educational attainment, difficulties at school and home, long periods without a job, care responsibilities with insufficient support for also doing something else, having English as an additional language and the experience of racial discrimination, and the disability or chronic illness of oneself or one's dependants.

Question 8 - Summary points

- There is evidence that offering financial incentives to adults can act as an effective spur to taking up training opportunities. This is in keeping with the evidence to emerge from initiatives targeted at younger people only, which also suggest that financial incentives do work.

- The ethos of support agencies, and the personal approach and attitudes of staff, can be critical to their success in engaging clients in training and learning opportunities. Evaluation of a voluntary sector training and employment initiative found clients particularly valued the caring, supportive and respectful attitude of staff. This was as true for young people taking part as for older adults.

- It is particularly important that agency staff recognise and understand the complexity of their clients' problems – and the barriers to participation that they face. Learners value a client-centred approach in which agency staff make explicit their belief in and commitment to clients being able to seize the opportunities on offer.

- It is not only those without work who need support. It can be particularly difficult for someone in a low-paid job to access careers advice, support or further training. This points to the need for in-work financial support to underpin any strategy that explicitly encourages people to take employment that is characterised by low income and high turnover.

Summary messages from current practice

Here we bring together some of the latest thinking about promising practice, by drawing out some key messages from the many reports we have received from local managers and practitioners working on NEET issues with children, young people and their families and with colleagues in their own and other agencies.

Inevitably, this is a snapshot only of the good work that is going on in local authority areas in England and Wales, and not all the documents we have drawn on will be located easily by those wanting to explore some of the ideas in more detail. We have tried to reduce this possible frustration for readers by referring to most local authorities by name. We hope this approach, combined with your own searching of the website of particular local children's services and Connexions, will prove helpful. The Department for Children, Schools and Families is committed to disseminating examples of good practice through its dedicated NEET website – www.dfes.gov.uk/14-19/neet The website will update you on NEET developments, including young people aged 18, about whom least progress has been made so far. The recent review, led by the Prime Minister's Delivery Unit, highlights some of the key challenges - the need to improve the tracking and segmentation of young people in this age group; clear roles and responsibilities between different agencies and better data sharing between Jobcentre Plus and Connexions; and high quality information, advice and guidance and better engagement of employers to meet the demand for work-based learning places.

A striking overall message from work at the three levels we cover below – strategic, operational and practitioner – is that 'stuff happens' when the work is being done by or with the support of local champions. These are people who are inspired to make a difference to the life chances of young people moving on to the next stage of life, and who set out to tackle that challenge with energy and a creative spirit, while paying careful heed to the messages from children and families about what will work best for them and why.

at strategic level

Provide clear vision and leadership

- Having one shared aim can help address the problems of different thresholds for services because it highlights particular issues that need tackling as a priority by health, education and social care. One of three common targets across agencies was reducing the number of young people NEET (Brighton & Hove).
- Think 'common' – with the same simple target figures, eg everyone working to 9 per cent (Barnsley), or the same clear

outcomes (Manchester).

- Help everyone see the work as a priority for them, by working through 14-19 clusters and by making use of strategic leads to get issues on everyone's agendas.

- Get ownership. Offering the top five NEET local schools extra support enabled governors and head teachers to become more engaged in the work needed, as did having a NEET prevention guide for schools and an action plan for each site (Manchester).

- Make representations beyond your immediate network about the issues that frustrate your staff. For example, alert government to the problems created by unhelpful benefit rules, to the need to focus on young people's welfare and sense of worth as well as national targets, and to the unhelpful duplication involved in reporting to one department about a young person as a care leaver and to another on their NEET status (Dorset). Work via a NEET improvement team across your Government Office area (Manchester).

Have a strategy that fits your local structure (and vice-versa)

- Make sure the NEET work is part of implementation of Common Assessment Framework assessment and planning, the allocation of Lead Professionals and the work of Teams Around the Child (Bournemouth, Greenwich).

- Think about locating NEET work in the local authority's Economic Well-being Team, to foster links with regeneration and urban renewal issues (Manchester).

- Ensure that your thorough needs analysis feeds into careful commissioning of contracts with the voluntary, statutory and community sectors (Hammersmith and Fulham).

- Think about how to make best use of the structures already in place, eg the NEETs Hotspot pilot was developed from within the Lifelong Learning Theme Group (one of ten local theme groups) and when a part-time NEETs worker was appointed for the pilot he was plugged into the theme group network immediately and operational within hours (Barnsley).

Focus on success

- Put a positive spin on what you're doing – which is raising participation, rather than simply reducing figures about NEET. Talk about increasing 'young people in learning 16 to 18' (Durham). Set up a Successful Young People Board rather than a NEET Strategy Group (Sandwell).

- Use a 'passport to success', a £10 incentive that helps young people bring together different bits of their learning (Hull).

- Promote what has been achieved on the back of previous target setting – eg 100 per cent of care leavers are in suitable accommodation (Nottinghamshire).
- Convey the gains for everyone of good joint work – and use publicity that is upbeat, eg about locality networks: 'It's a network that's quite easy to become part of, to contribute to, and to gain benefit from' (Barnsley).
- Focus on what will attract young people to want to succeed – eg encourage schools to branch out into other work, do outreach, run with the times (Cheshire).
- Engage with the media to harness their help in disseminating your successes and your plans for responding holistically to young people and families, and to expand the coverage beyond a narrow focus on standards and targets.
- Get to the heart of what a policy intends to achieve – young people need more that an 'offer' of a place in EET, they need the offer to become a sustained place in post-16 provision.

Pool budgets

- Do this across the local authority (Hull).
- Or to facilitate joint work in particular areas or departments, eg in neighbourhood renewal, for NEET Hotspot pilot work (Manchester).

Act as a good parent

- Provide jobs within the local authority for local young people (Greenwich).
- Extend this approach for children leaving care to other young residents in each ward or neighbourhood.
- Be proud of acting as a good parent – eg promoting work placements and jobs as part of helping develop 'the family business' (Dorset); promoting the Top 700, a project to provide, in each of the seven council areas, 100 jobs for 100 young people, working with the most persistent absentees from school (Hull).

Include young people

- Involve them in the monitoring returns to the Learning and Skills Council on the Key Stage 4 Engagement Programme (Bournemouth).
- Include all your local young people – those in custody are not available for the labour market at present, but some will be serving very short sentences, and you need to be planning for them as well as for young people still on your patch and so more visible (Bournemouth).

Engage with local academics

- Local higher education colleagues might help conduct research to analyse and understand the risk factors for young people being NEET in your area (Bournemouth).

at operational level

Think small and regular

- Enable people to focus attention on particular issues and young people, and to provide regular and detailed reporting on the progress or problems to resolve, eg set a target of acquiring six new tenancies per year for children leaving care (Bournemouth). Divide the local authority area into small sections where staff can take on responsibility for their 'own' young people (Hull).

- Use task groups to meet every two or three weeks to review progress and commission immediate activities or interventions, eg for planning the September guarantee, have someone from the local authority, the LSC and Connexions (Nottinghamshire).

- Encourage regular reviews of work, eg the transition worker does a monthly review of both her caseload and the work coming through the drop-in sessions, to ensure that new issues are being covered (Monmouthshire).

Be pro-active and problem solve

- Take the view that social inclusion for pupils should be about good quality, effective prevention rather than well-managed school exclusion (Sefton).

- Identify and act on the reasons why some local children have a history of chronic school non-attendance (Blackpool).

- Work on a different way of recording information rather than persist with the problems of the old system (Brighton & Hove).

- Help staff manage their caseloads, eg prioritise the NEET work into three bands of severity of need and use change management techniques to help embed the new procedures (Nottinghamshire).

- Know the scene – ask for daily updates on work with particular young people, take an interest in how staff are working creatively (Hull, Durham).

- Employ dedicated personal advisers to work with young people in particular circumstances, eg teenage parents, young offenders and those from BME backgrounds (Hammersmith and Fulham).

- Employ staff who have real expectations for young people and are committed to finding ways of improving their life chances (Cheshire).

Give staff tools for their work

- Put out a weekly bulletin of activities and opportunities for young people so each team has a directory to use in their work (Greenwich).
- Spend your budget rather than holding on until the year end (Dorset).
- Give locality teams regular and detailed data about young people, so they stay up to date about progress being made (Barnsley).
- Be clear about where you want the balance to lie between direct work and procedural work, eg use a young person's right to an early interview to help staff manage their time, and to get partners held to account (Manchester). Find ways of supporting staff to see every young person and then referring them on rather than spending undue time developing protocols for service thresholds (Monmouthshire).
- Ensure that staff can make best use of the skills around them. Encourage them to work with local and national voluntary sector organisations (Southwark). Use local recruitment agency expertise or staff to work out ways of engaging with potential employers (Greenwich). Think about mixed staff teams, including teachers, social workers, youth workers (Nottinghamshire).

Make it easy for young people

- Pay them £5 for travel to a quarterly meeting with potential employers who can offer a job or a job interview at once (Greenwich).
- Have a common application process linked to the 14-19 prospectus (Barnsley).
- Develop flexible start dates for taking up new opportunities (Durham, Cornwall and Devon).
- Increase the provision of activities over the summer to retain interest and provide follow-up work to encourage young people to take up offers (Nottinghamshire).
- Provide multiagency support, including GP/nurse services, from a One Stop Shop where those with particular EET needs feel safe to access help from both universal and targeted services (Hammersmith and Fulham).
- Use outreach community sessions in areas of high NEET need, to get to young people and their families and friends (Sandwell). Do door-knocking and home visits to try and excite residents about EET possibilities (Nottinghamshire).

at practitioner level

Doing what it takes with young people

- Make sure you're committed to not giving up on young people, and to tracking intensively their progress – and that of potential work and training providers – until an appropriate 'offer' is not just made but also delivered (Nottinghamshire).

- Create opportunities to motivate young people, eg by organising motivational residential meetings to open up more options for the future for young people unwilling to travel out of their area (Greenwich). Enthuse young people to take steps forward on the things that interest them, even if those are not directly related to EET status (Monmouthshire).

Doing what it takes with families

- Make sure you have the skills to engage with young people's families, including having a sound understanding of where they are at and being able to talk to some of them about their entrenched thinking (Cheshire).

Working with others

- Harness those around you to join you in your work, as advocates or ambassadors to support individual young people make and act on choices (Nottinghamshire).

- Record for a purpose, using your assessment work with young people and their families to clarify the time you will need to allocate to them and to decide who else can help provide what's needed (Monmouthshire).

some of the key studies about young people

Community programmes for disaffected young people

1 from list of references starting on page 99

location
The 40 most deprived local authority areas, England.

NEET issue
An evaluation of the Neighbourhood Support Fund, a six-year government project designed to help disaffected young people (aged 13 to 19) take the first step back into an activity that might spark off an interest and make it more likely that they would move on to education, employment or training.

study features
Large-scale national evaluation – 665 projects, most managed by the Community Development Foundation (CDF), who helped local community organisations set up and deliver local programmes. Young people were attracted via friends and community networks, using informal activities such as sport, computers and DJ-ing. It involved just under 50,000 young people (60 per cent were older teenagers, ie, aged 15 to 19; it's not clear how many were 16 to 18).

methodology
Questionnaires at the start and end of involvement – over 4,000 interviews with staff and young people, focus groups, and case studies (examples of local developments, tracking and commenting on activity and progress). Used comparison groups, from projects undertaken by the Prince's Trust and two other CDF studies. The aim was to evaluate hard or positional outcomes (education and jobs) and soft or primary outcomes (socialisation, confidence, the 'distance travelled' towards getting work or qualifications).

key findings and/or conclusions
- The scheme attracted disadvantaged young people, including those affected by school exclusion, offending behaviour, substance misuse and homelessness.

- Young people in the programmes had similar aspirations to other young people – when asked what was most important to them, the most common response was their 'family' and 'an interesting job'.

- When signed-off by their local scheme, 71 per cent of the full cohort were recorded as having a 'positive outcome' in terms of education, employment or training. (Note – some of these outcomes are more robust than others (in the sense of being about change rather than an output) eg, gaining experience or skills as opposed to being referred to a personal adviser.)

- There were gains in softer (primary) outcomes such as confidence, self-esteem and improved communication skills. Young people felt more secure when given the opportunity for gradual involvement in new activities.

- There were reported gains for organisations and communities too – including fresh involvement by young people and their families and friends, new topics and resources, and involvement in other community ventures.

- Programmes were deemed effective in reducing inter-generational tension, through bringing older and younger people in contact, but not in reducing ethnic divisions within communities.

- The average cost was £1,000 per young person.

Cognitive and non-cognitive skills

9 from list of references starting on page 99

location
England, Scotland and Wales.

NEET issue
To consider the policy implications arising from the links, if any, between the development of early cognitive and non-cognitive skills and children's experiences at home and school.

study features
A quantitative analysis of data from the National Child Development Study, which includes detailed longitudinal records for all children born in Great Britain in one week in 1958 (and followed up every 5 to 10 years since then).

methodology
This study drew on data about the children and their families at age 0, 7, 11, 16 and 42. The data included teacher assessment of children's abilities and validated scales to measure social maladjustment and depression. The factors analysed include both sets of skills (cognitive and non-cognitive), school attainment, work status, behaviour, family background, and home learning environment; 12 domains are used to explore non-cognitive (social) skills. The outcomes used to analyse behaviour include smoking, truancy, school exclusion, crime and teenage parenthood.

key findings and/or conclusions
- Social skills are more malleable than cognitive skills in children aged 7 to 11, highlighting the need for early attention to social skills at this age.
- Some social skills are particularly important for positive outcomes – especially self-discipline, perseverance and concentration.
- Social adjustment is important for young people remaining in education after age 16, with truancy exerting the strongest influence on outcomes.
- Parental reading and interest in th child's education makes a positive difference, with parental problem. having an adverse impact.
- There is a strong association betw depression at age 11 and 42, highlighting the need for early attention here too.
- The researchers conclude that soc skills have an impact on both educational attainment and beha that puts young people at risk of s exclusion.

Using sport and leisure to wider young people's horizons

16 from list of references starting on page 99

location
The most deprived local neighbourhoo in England and Wales.

NEET issue
Learning lessons from Positive Futures social inclusion programme that used s and leisure activities as a means of motivating disaffected young people, especially those deemed to be at risk o antisocial or offending behaviour or substance misuse. The intention behin the programme was to enable young people to talk to responsible adults ab issues affecting their life and so gain access to lifestyle, education and employment opportunities that will wi their horizons and have a positive imp on their behaviour.

study features
An evaluation of the six-year programr for young people aged 10 to 16, that ra 100+ local areas. The report includes useful information about different rese methods and the dilemmas in measuri progress towards outcomes.

methodology

The study focuses on the second half of the six-year programme. It is a two-year research project exploring the themes arising from the local activities. It opts for using six case studies, rather than quantitative research methods, to explore the common themes arising – about what helps to make a difference to young people's lives, ways of engaging them, and the ethos needed by organisations doing such work.

key findings and/or conclusions

- Activities are seen as a good basis for establishing relationships with young people who feel alienated from mainstream agencies and authority figures.

- They are also a useful vehicle for enabling discussion between young people and responsible adults.

- This can help influence young people's behaviour by widening their horizons and helping them access new opportunities and gain more control over decisions about their future.

- The most successful sport-related programmes and projects are those that are realistic about what is achievable and work clearly within those parameters.

- What is important is not the sport or other activity itself but finding what will attract and engage individual young people. Projects with a range of activities are more successful than those using sport alone.

- Organisations working with young people need to have the flexibility to innovate, take risks, work outside normal structures, and be managed by people with direct experience of youth work.

- Outreach work and approaches that stimulate personal development are more likely to enable workers to gain the trust of young people.

- Evaluation is important, to build up the evidence about what works and how and for whom. Questions that probe how programmes engage and enthuse young people are as instructive as collecting statistical data about project activity.

Using non-formal learning Awards to prepare young people for work

38 from list of references starting on page 99

location

Eight local authority areas in England.

NEET issue

A study to test the value of using non-formal Awards (like the Duke of Edinburgh's Award and UK Youth) to deliver some of the content of the government's Entry to Employment (E2E) programme, which is designed to help young people be ready for moving into employment. Nationally, there are about 40 such Award schemes that accredit young people's achievements and learning.

study features

A two-year action research project covering eight Award programmes, one in each geographical area, and involving 2,400 young people aged 16 to 18, linked to one of 70 delivery centres in the pilot. This included some schemes developed for teenage mothers. On average, the Award programmes offered activity for four of the 16 hours per week allocated to the E2E programme.

methodology

Questionnaires, interviews with young people and providers, scrutiny of young people's plans, and case studies to track activity and progress. The main outcome being tested was whether use of the Award programmes provided a positive progression route. This was defined as the acquisition of qualifications while on E2E or, for those leaving E2E, entry to work, further education or further work-based learning such as an Apprenticeship.

key findings and/or conclusions

- Awards offer a useful framework for delivering (and accrediting) the three strands of E2E. They were used for the personal and social development strand by half the providers in the study, for the vocational strand by a third of providers, and for the basic skills strand by a quarter.

- There was a strong indication that Awards improved the rate of entry to employment, education or training – 46 per cent of those on the Award scheme as part of E2E achieved this, compared with 38 per cent of those on E2E overall.

- The main gains for young people were about recognising their own achievement, self-esteem and self-confidence, and skills in working in groups.

- The Awards were also used, in half the areas, for the E2E strand of delivering vocational skills.

- A positive aspect of the schemes was their value in motivating young people, identifying discrete and small achievements, and providing a way of measuring and validating that progress.

- The method of delivery was important – direct delivery by those running the Award was preferable but more costly than using other people. Guidance for other people needs to focus on training, support, how to get going and keep going, maintaining quality, having sufficient staff time, and adapting the award to ensure a good fit with the E2E programme.

- The researchers present a strong case for these Awards becoming embedded into mainstream pre-employment programmes.

Skills in literacy, numeracy and language

46 from list of references starting on page 99

location
England and Wales.

NEET issue
To research and develop a training strategy and training materials that would improve young people's skills in literacy, language and numeracy.

study features
This was a 15-month project. This study reports on the action research conducted in the first seven months, which aimed to identify local practices and resources used to help young people develop their basic skills, and to consider the barriers to young people's progress – and then use that knowledge to produce a framework of critical success factors to inform the final product (the training strategy and materials). The report includes a literature review on social exclusion, research studies about basic skills and theories of informal education.

methodology
A postal questionnaire (58 returns from 300 local organisations offering learning in community centres, shop units, schools and colleges), 25 project visits, phone discussion with these and others, an email discussion group, and eight case studies exploring the resources available locally and ways of engaging young people whose 'learning has to compete with life'.

key findings and/or conclusions

- Common barriers to young people's learning included negative experiences of school, substance misuse problems and a lifestyle marked by trauma, lack of consistency and fear of dealing with new people or experiences. Most had left school without qualifications and up to a third had behaviour problems associated with undiagnosed dyslexia, ADHD or unresolved anger.

- Success was more likely if organisations could engage effectively with young people, used publicity that was deemed credible and used ICT as a training method.

- Engaging young people was more likely to be achieved if an informal approach was used, embedding basic skills in learning about interesting topics, with young people praised for their progress and taught by empathetic staff.

- The short-term and temporary funding of most schemes led to uncertainty and anxiety about the work and clashed with the important aim of developing relationships with young people. An additional tension was between the focus on engaging and motivating young people (soft outcomes) and the funding that was generally linked to targets and accreditation (hard outcomes).

- The need to connect with young people 'on the edge' makes the ethos of youth work particularly valuable for this sort of work. Guidance might usefully help youth workers draw on the specialist skills needed for teaching these basic skills.

- Key aspects of the framework to inform the training strategy were about the importance of engaging and sustaining young people's interest, promoting strong relationships between young people and adults, and using appropriate teaching methods to deliver literacy, language and numeracy.

Participation in organised non-formal activities out of school

63 from list of references starting on page 99

location
SW England.

NEET issue
To test the assumption that positive relationships between teachers and pupils require them to have highly developed interpersonal skills, and that young people can develop these skills through opportunities to participate in organised, non-formal activities out of school.

study features
Small-scale local study – 55 children, aged 11 (primary) or 14 (secondary), from urban and rural schools in a relatively deprived area; 22 on free school meals (poorer), 30 not on free school meals (richer).

methodology
Children mapped their evening and weekend activities and were then interviewed about which activities they did and why, the cost involved, their relationships with other participants, what they learnt and how, and perceived connection between the activity and their learning in school.

key findings and/or conclusions
- The benefits for participants included self-confidence, acquiring new skills that were valued by themselves and others, learning alongside enthusiastic adults, peer friendships and fun.

- Only half of the poorer children participated, compared with four-fifths of the richer ones.

- The obstacles to participation included fees and travel costs, limited knowledge of activities, lack of confidence in accessing them, and a perception that activities were not for them.

- Parental support was a key factor in children's participation.

- Children want local activities that are open to everyone (parks, playgrounds, swimming pools) and so avoid a sense of stigma, and more specialist activities that are broad in scope, eg, art activities (not just sport).

- The researchers conclude that participation does bring a positive spin-off in learning in school. (Note – the evidence presented in support of this assertion is not strong.)

references

1 Bailey G (2006) *The Neighbourhood Support Fund: Final evaluation report.* London: Community Development Foundation

2 Bamfield L (2007) *The Contribution of Non-formal Learning to Young People's Life Chances.* A Fabian Society report for The National Youth Agency. Leicester: NYA
Online version available at
www.nya.org.uk/shared_asp_files/gfsr.asp?nodeid=110385

3 Barnes T and Stiasny M (1995) *Mentoring: Making it work.* Southampton: Bassett Press

4 Bazalgette J (1971) *Freedom, Authority and the Young Adult.* London: Pitman Medical Publishing Co.

5 Bentley T and Gurumurthy R (1999) *Destination Unknown – Engaging with the problems of marginalised youth.* London: Demos

6 Bercow J (2008) *The Bercow Report. A review of services for children and young people (0-19) with speech, language and communication needs.* Nottingham: DCSF Publications
Online version available at
www.dcsf.gov.uk/bercowreview/docs/7771-DCSF-BERCOW.PDF

7 Cann J, Falshaw L, Nugent F and Friendship C (2003) *Understanding What Works: Accredited cognitive skills programmes for adult men and young offenders.* (Home Office Findings 226.) London: Home Office

8 Carnegie UK Trust (2008) *Empowering Young People. The final report of the Carnegie young people initiative.* Dunfermline: Carnegie UK Trust
Online version available at
http://cypi.carnegieuktrust.org.uk/files/cypi_final_report_0.pdf

9 Carneiro P, Crawford C and Goodman A (2007) *The Impact of Early Cognitive and Non-cognitive Skills on Later Outcomes.* London: Centre for the Economics of Education, London School of Economics
Online version available at
http://cee.lse.ac.uk/cee%20dps/ceedp92.pdf

10 Chell P (2008) 'Moving Healthy FE Forward' *Further Education In Brief* (June) e-newsletter published online at
www.healthyschools.gov.uk/Uploads/Users/National%20Co-ordinators/ice-stuart/NHSP%20FE%20inBrief%20June%202008.pdf

11 Coles B (2000) *Joined-up Youth Research, Policy and Practice: An agenda for change?* Leicester: Youth Work Press

12 Coles B, Hutton S, Bradshaw J, Craig G, Godfrey C and Johnson J (2002) *Literature Review of the Costs of Being 'Not in Education, Employment or Training' at Age 16-18.* (DfES Research Report 347.) London: DfES
Online version available at
www.dcsf.gov.uk/research/data/uploadfiles/RR347.pdf

13 Colley H (2006) *Mentoring for Young People Not in Education, Employment or Training: A 'NEET' solution, but to whose problems?* (Nuffield Review of 14-19 Education and Training Working Paper 36). Oxford: The Nuffield Review, Department of Education
Online version available at
www.nuffield14-19review.org.uk/files/documents121-1.pdf

14 Community Development Foundation (2007) *Community Organisations and Young People – The benefits of working together. Summary of the NSF evaluation and programme.* London: CDF
Online version available at
www.cdf.org.uk/SITE/UPLOAD/DOCUMENT/NSFforwebsite.pdf

15 Copps J, Sandford S and Yeowart C (2007) *Lean On Me: Mentoring for young people at risk. A guide for donors and funders.* London: New Philanthropy Capital
Online version available at
www.philanthropycapital.org/research/research_reports/education/mentoring.aspx

16 Crabbe T, with Bailey G, Blackshaw T, Brown A, Choak C, Gidley B, Mellor G, O'Connor K, Slater I and Woodhouse D (2006) *Knowing the Score. Positive Futures Case Study Research: Final report.* Manchester: Substance
Online version available at
www.substance.coop/files/knowing_the_score.pdf

17 Dench S (2007) *Impact of Care to Learn: Tracking the destinations of young parents funded in 2003-04.* Brighton: Institute for Employment Studies
Online version available at
http://caretolearn.lsc.gov.uk/evaluation/

18 Dench S and Bellis A (2007) *Learning for Young Mothers: A qualitative study of flexible provision.* Brighton: Institute for Employment Studies
Online version available at
http://caretolearn.lsc.gov.uk/evaluation/

19 Department for Children, Schools and Families (2007) *Raising Expectations: Staying in education and training post-16. From policy to legislation.* Nottingham: DCSF Publications
Available online at
www.dcsf.gov.uk/14-19/documents/Raising%20Expectations.pdf

20 Department for Children, Schools and Families (2008) *Promoting Achievement, Valuing Success: A strategy for 14-19 qualifications.* Norwich: The Stationery Office (Cm 7354)
Online version available at
www.dcsf.gov.uk/publications/14-19qualifications/pdfs/14-13 Qualifications.pdf

21 Department for Children, Schools and Families (2008) *Reducing the Number of Young People Not in Education, Employment or Training (NEET). The strategy.* (Strategy launched November 2007, printed copies available 2008) Nottingham: DCSF Publications
Online version available at
www.dcsf.gov.uk/14-19/documents/neet_strategy_0803.pdf

See also the NEET Toolkit (2008), practical guidance that underpins the Strategy
Online version available at
www.dcsf.gov.uk/14-19/documents/7508-DCSF-Neet%20Toolkit.pdf

22 Department for Children, Schools and Families (2008) *Youth Taskforce Action Plan*. Nottingham: DCSF Publications
Online version available at
www.everychildmatters.gov.uk/_files/YouthTaskActionPlan.pdf

23 Department for Children, Schools and Families/National Statistics (2008) *Participation in Education, Training and Employment by 16-18 Year Olds in England*. (Statistical First Release 13/2008.) London: DCSF
Online version available at
www.dcsf.gov.uk/rsgateway/DB/SFR/s000792/SFR_132008.pdf

24 Department for Education and Skills (2007) *Care Matters: Time for change*. London: The Stationery Office (Cm 7137)
Online version available at
www.dcsf.gov.uk/publications/timeforchange/docs/timeforchange.pdf

25 Department for Innovation, Universities & Skills (2007) *World Class Skills: Implementing the Leitch Review of skills in England*. Norwich: The Stationery Office (Cm 7181)
Online version available at
www.dcsf.gov.uk/skillsstrategy/uploads/documents/World%20Class%2
0Skills%20FINAL.pdf

26 Department of Health and Department for Children, Schools and Families (2007) *Teenage Parents Next Steps: Guidance for local authorities and primary care trusts*. Nottingham: DCSF Publications
Online version available at
www.everychildmatters.gov.uk/_files/6983570B080FA8B58C9CF31C58
547A7D.pdf

27 Employment Support Unit (2000) *Mentoring Young People: Lessons from Youthstart*. Birmingham: ESU

28 Evans H (2001) *Sprouting Seeds. Outcomes from a community-based employment programme*. London: ESRC Research Centre for Analysis of Social Exclusion, London School of Economics
Online version available at
http://sticerd.lse.ac.uk/dps/case/cr/CASEreport7.pdf

29 Gaskell C (2008) *Kids Company Helps with the Whole Problem. Research and evaluation programme*. London: Queen Mary, University of London

30 Golden S and Sims D (1997) *Review of Industrial Mentoring in Schools*. Slough: National Foundation for Educational Research

31 Golden S, Spielhofer T, Sims D and O'Donnell L (2004) *Supporting the Hardest-to-reach Young People: The contribution of the Neighbourhood Support Fund*. (DfES Research Report 535.) Nottingham: DfES Publications
Online version available at
www.dfes.gov.uk/research/data/uploadfiles/RR535.pdf

32 Hartley R (2006) *Churn Amongst NEET Young People in Cornwall and Devon.* Connexions in Cornwall and Devon Ltd.

33 Hartley R (2006) *NEETs in Cornwall and Devon.* Connexions Cornwall and Devon Ltd.

34 HM Treasury (2003) *Every Child Matters.* London: The Stationery Office (Cm 5860)
Online version available at
www.everychildmatters.gov.uk/_files/EBE7EEAC90382663E0D5BBF24 C99A7AC.pdf

35 HM Treasury and Department for Education and Skills (2007) *Aiming High for Disabled Children: Better support for families.* Norwich: Office of Public Sector Information
Online version available at
www.hm-treasury.gov.uk/media/C/2/cyp_disabledchildren180507.pdf

36 Hoggarth L and Smith D (2004) *Understanding the Impact of Connexions on Young People at Risk.* (Research Report RR607.) Nottingham: DfES Publications
Online version available at
www.dcsf.gov.uk/research/data/uploadfiles/RR607.pdf

37 House of Lords Select Committee on Economic Affairs (2007) *Apprenticeship: A key route to skill.* London: The Stationery Office
Online version available at:
www.publications.parliament.uk/pa/ld200607/ldselect/ldeconaf /ldeconaf.htm

38 Jessiman T, Loewenstein P and Long A (2005) *The Positive Contribution of Non-formal Awards to Learning. Final report on the Action Research project on the contribution of non-formal Awards to Entry to Employment.* Leicester: The National Youth Agency

39 Johnson C, Newton B, Usher T and Hillage J (2008) *Activity and Learning Agreements Pilot. Programme Theory Evaluation. Working paper 1: Incentivising participation in Activity Agreements.* (Working paper RW028.) London: Department for Children, Schools and Families
Online version available at
www.dcsf.gov.uk/research/data/uploadfiles/DCSF-RW028.pdf

40 Johnson C, Page R and Munro M (2008) *Activity and Learning Agreements Pilot. Programme Theory Evaluation. Working paper 2: Signing up to a Learning Agreement.* (Working paper RW029.) London: Department for Children, Schools and Families
Online version available at
www.dcsf.gov.uk/research/data/uploadfiles/DCSF-RW029.pdf

41 Johnston L, MacDonald R, Mason P, Ridley L and Webster C (2000) *Snakes and Ladders: Young people, transitions and social exclusion.* Bristol/York: The Policy Press/Joseph Rowntree Foundation

42 Jones G (2002) *The Youth Divide: Diverging paths to adulthood.* York: Joseph Rowntree Foundation
Online version available at
www.jrf.org.uk/bookshop/eBooks/1842630814.pdf

43 Jones G (undated) *Enjoying and Achieving: The implications for youth work of Every Child Matters. (Book 4 of The Contribution of Youth Work to the Every Child Matters Outcomes)*
Published online by The National Youth Agency at
www.nya.org.uk/information/100584/researchpublications
(checked 1 September 2008)

44 Kendall S, Johnson A, Gulliver C, Martin K and Kinder K (2004) *Evaluation of the Vulnerable Children Grant. (DfES Research Report 592.)* London: DfES
Online version available at
www.dcsf.gov.uk/research/data/uploadfiles/RR592.pdf

45 McNally S and Telhaj S (2007) *The Cost of Exclusion: Counting the cost of youth exclusion in the UK.* London: Prince's Trust
Online version available at
www.princes-trust.org.uk/main site v2/downloads/Cost of Exclusion apr07.pdf

46 McNeil B and Smith L (2004) *Success Factors in Informal Learning: Young adults' experience of literacy, language and numeracy. Progress report.* London: National Research and Development Centre for adult literacy and numeracy, Institute of Education.
Online version available at
www.nrdc.org.uk/publications_details.asp?ID=40

47 Maguire S, Thompson J, Hillage J, Dewson S, Miller L, Johnson C, Newton B, Bates P and Page P (2008) *Evaluation of the Activity and Learning Agreements Pilot. Process Evaluation: Year one report. (DCSF Research Report DCSF-RW027.)* London: DCSF
Online version available at
www.dcsf.gov.uk/research/data/uploadfiles/DCSF-RW027.pdf

48 Margo J and Dixon M with Pearce N and Reed H (2006) *Freedom's Orphans: Raising youth in a changing world.* London: Institute for Public Policy Research

49 National Audit Office (2004) *Connexions Service: Advice and guidance for all young people. Report by the Comptroller and Auditor General HC 484 Session 2003-2004.* London: The Stationery Office
Online version available at
www.nao.org.uk/publications/nao_reports/03-04/0304484.pdf

50 The National Youth Agency and The Fabian Society (2008) *The Contribution of Non-formal Learning to Young People's Life Chances – Executive summary.* Leicester: The National Youth Agency
Online version available at
www.nya.org.uk/shared_asp_files/GFSR.asp?NodeID=110333

51 Nice K, Irvine A and Sainsbury R (2008) *Pathways to Work from Incapacity Benefits: A study of experience and use of the Job Preparation Premium.* (Research Report 474.) Norwich: HMSO
Online version available at
www.dwp.gov.uk/asd/asd5/rports2007-2008/rrep474.pdf

52 Office of the Deputy Prime Minister (2004) *The Impact of Government Policy on Social Exclusion among Young People: A review of the literature for the Social Exclusion Unit in the Breaking the Cycle series.* London: ODPM
Online version available at
www.cabinetoffice.gov.uk/ffi/media/assets/www.cabinetoffice.gov.uk
/social_exclusion_task_force/publications_1997_to_2006
/impact_young_people%20pdf.ashx

53 Office of the Deputy Prime Minister (2005) *Transitions. Young Adults with Complex Needs. A Social Exclusion Unit final report.* London: ODPM
Online version available at
www.cabinetoffice.gov.uk/ffi/media/assets/www.cabinetoffice.gov.uk
/social_exclusion_task_force/publications_1997_to_2006
/transitions_young_adults%20pdf.ashx

54 Ofsted (1999) *Raising the Attainment of Minority Ethnic Pupils: School and LEA responses.* (HMI 170). London: Ofsted
Online version available at
www.ofsted.gov.uk/content/download/5984/54320/file
/RaisingtheattainmentofminorityethnicPupils_schoolandLEAresponses.pdf

55 Organisation for Economic Co-operation and Development (2008) *Jobs for Youth: United Kingdom.* Paris: OECD
Online version available at
www.oecd.org/document/25/0,3343,en_2649_34747_40841177_1_1_1_
1,00.html

56 Payne J (2002) *Attitudes to Education and Choices at Age 16: A brief research review. Report to the DfES Advisory Panel on Research Issues for the 14-19 age group.* London: Policy Studies Institute

57 Rennison J, Maguire S, Middleton S and Ashworth K (2005) *People Not in Education, Employment or Training: Evidence from the Education Maintenance Allowance Pilots Database.* (DfES Research Report 628.) Nottingham: DfES Publications
Online version available at
www.dfes.gov.uk/research/data/uploadfiles/RR628.pdf

58 Sachdev D, Harries B and Roberts T (2006) *Regional and Sub-regional Variation in NEETs – Reasons, remedies and impact.* London: Learning and Skills Development Agency
Online version available at
www.lsneducation.org.uk/research/files/RCFdemandLearning/NEET_re
port.pdf

59 Social Exclusion Unit (1999) *Bridging the Gap: New opportunities for 16-18 year olds not in education, employment or training.* London: Cabinet Office (Cm 4405)
Online version available at
www.cabinetoffice.gov.uk/ffi/media/assets/www.cabinetoffice.gov.uk
/social_exclusion_task_force/publications_1997_to_2006/bridging_gap
%20pdf.ashx

60 Tikly L, Caballero C, Haynes J and Hill J (2004) *Understanding the Educational Needs of Mixed Heritage Pupils.* (DfES Research Report RR549.) Nottingham: DfES Publications
Online version available at
www.standards.dfes.gov.uk/ethnicminorities/resources
/RR549_June04.pdf

61 Training Standards Council (2000) *Modern Apprenticeships: A survey report by the Training Standards Council.* London: TSC

62 Webster C, Simpson D, MacDonald R, Abbas A, Cieslik M, Shildrick T and Simpson M (2004) *Poor Transitions: Social exclusion and young adults.* Bristol: Policy Press in association with Joseph Rowntree Foundation
Online version available at
www.jrf.org.uk/bookshop/eBooks/1861347340.pdf

63 Wikeley F, Bullock K, Muschamp Y and Ridge T (2007) *Educational Relationships Outside School: Why access is important.* York: Joseph Rowntree Foundation
Online version available at
www.jrf.org.uk/bookshop/eBooks/2027-education-poverty-
activities.pdf

64 York Consulting Ltd (2005) *Literature Review of the NEET Group.* Edinburgh: Scottish Executive Social Research
Online version available at
www.scotland.gov.uk/Resource/Doc/77843/0018812.pdf

65 Young Adults Learning Partnership (2006) *Learning from the Edge: Engaging and motivating young adults – A review of policy and practice, 1997-2007.* Leicester: YALP

66 Youth Justice Board (2006) *Barriers to Engagement in Education, Training and Employment.* London: Youth Justice Board for England and Wales
Online version available at
www.yjb.gov.uk/Publications/Scripts/prodView.asp?idproduct=291&eP

67 Youth Justice Board (2007) *Keeping Young People Engaged. A summary of an evaluation of the Keeping Young People Engaged education, training and employment project.* London: Youth Justice Board
Online version available at
www.yjb.gov.uk/publications/Scripts/prodView.asp?idProduct=348&eP=

68 UNICEF (2007) *Child Poverty in Perspective: An overview of child well-being in rich countries.* Florence: UNICEF, Innocenti Research Centre
Online version available at
http://unicef-icdc.org/publications/pdf/rc7_eng.pdf

appendix

How the UK compares to other countries

- Historically, the UK has had low participation rates in education and training, with one of the lowest levels of participation in post-16 education in Europe [48].

- In the most recent comparison, the UK was 24th out of 30 on the rate of participation of 17-year-olds, compared to other countries in the Organisation for Economic Cooperation and Development (OECD) [55].

- The UK has a low ranking internationally on various indicators of young people's performance, productivity and social inclusion [68].

- The percentage of young adults in the UK with low-level or no qualifications compares very unfavourably to France (for all age ranges) and to Germany (for those aged 25 to 28) [65].

- In sharp contrast with the UK, most European countries use apprenticeships as the main route by which almost half of their young people acquire vocational skills. The rate of continuity varies too – only 53 per cent of learners finish their apprenticeship here, compared with 75 per cent in Germany [65].

- Unlike young people in the rest of Europe, those in the UK have in the past been mainly self-supporting – dependent on their own earnings rather than on welfare or family support [43].

- One in five children in Britain is growing up in a workless household, a higher figure than in any other OECD country [43].

- Though the UK has moved closer to the European average, in 2005 child poverty rates were more than six times higher than in Denmark, nearly four times higher than in Sweden and more than double those of France [48].

- In a 2001-02 survey, just under 45 per cent of 12-year-old boys and 56 per cent of 12-year-old girls in England said they found their peers kind and helpful – far less than in any other European country (although Scotland and Ireland fared better). They were also more likely to have been involved in a fight with peers [48].

- In 2003, the UK had the highest rate of live births to teenagers in the 25 countries of the European Union – nearly one-fifth higher than Latvia (the next highest), and more than four times as high as Cyprus, Slovenia, Sweden and Denmark [48].

index

about the authors

Jo Tunnard has a background in teaching and the national voluntary sector, and works as an independent researcher, writer and editor. She is a founder member of rtb. Current work relates to the health, mental health and social care needs of young people and families in contact with the youth justice system, and evaluation of the pilot Family Drugs and Alcohol Court in central London. www.ryantunnardbrown.com

Tim Barnes is a freelance evaluator and researcher who set up a small consultancy Thinking for a Living in 1998 having spent 16 years training youth workers and teachers. He has a long-term interest in marginalised young people. He has set up and run youth unemployment and alternative to custody projects. More recently he has researched children missing from school and young people who disengage from learning.

Steve Flood is a freelance writer and editor who specialises in the field of children's services. He was editor of YoungMinds Magazine from 1995 until 2003.

about **The National Youth Agency**

Our mission is to support young people to achieve their full potential by working with organisations and services to improve the life chances of young people. We also work directly with young people themselves to develop their voice and influence in shaping policy and securing social justice. See our website: www.nya.org.uk for more information about our work.

about **research** in **practice**

research in practice is a department of The Dartington Hall Trust run in collaboration with the University of Sheffield, the Association of Directors of Children's Services and our network of over 100 Partner Agencies in England and Wales. Our mission is to promote positive outcomes for children and families through proper and greater use of research evidence. The work and methods of **research in practice** support the promotion of better outcomes for children and families through more effective, multiprofessional and multiagency collaborations, in part by creating and using reliable research evidence. More information is available on our website:

www.rip.org.uk from where our publications can also be purchased. Alternatively, contact our Dartington Office:

Blacklers, Park Road, Dartington, Totnes, Devon, TQ9 6EQ
t: 01803 867692 f: 01803 868816 e: ask@rip.org.uk

contributing to a sustainable future for children and families

research in practice aims to improve outcomes for vulnerable children and families in England and Wales by promoting and facilitating evidence-informed practice. To recognise our role as members of the wider global community, we will donate 25 per cent of the sale of this reveiw and our other publications to a designated international charitable project to support a sustainable future for children and families in need. Details of the project identified for support each year are on our website: www.rip.org.uk/charity